D0053636

THE
HOT ONE

A Memoir of Friendship, Sex, and Murder

CAROLYN MURNICK

Simon & Schuster

New York   London   Toronto   Sydney   New Delhi

Simon & Schuster
1230 Avenue of the Americas
New York, NY 10020

First Simon & Schuster hardcover edition August 2017

SIMON & SCHUSTER and colophon are
registered trademarks of Simon & Schuster, Inc.

For information about special discounts for bulk purchases,
please contact Simon & Schuster Special Sales at 1-866-506-1949
or business@simonandschuster.com.

The Simon & Schuster Speakers Bureau can bring authors to your live event.
For more information or to book an event contact the
Simon & Schuster Speakers Bureau at 1-866-248-3049
or visit our website at www.simonspeakers.com.

Interior design by Ruth Lee-Mui

Manufactured in the United States of America

1   3   5   7   9   10   8   6   4   2

Library of Congress Cataloging-in-Publication Data

Names: Murnick, Carolyn, author.
Title: The hot one : a memoir of friendship, sex, and murder / Carolyn Murnick.
Description: New York : Simon & Schuster, [2017]
Identifiers: LCCN 2016038744| ISBN 9781451625813 (hbk) | ISBN 9781451625820
(trade pbk) | ISBN 9781451625837 (ebook)
Subjects: LCSH: Murder—California—Los Angeles—Investigation—Case studies.
| Murder—California—Los Angeles—Case studies.
Classification: LCC HV6534.L7 M87 2017 | DDC 364.152/3092—dc23
LC record available at https://lccn.loc.gov/2016038744

ISBN 978-1-4516-2581-3
ISBN 978-1-4516-2583-7 (ebook)

For my parents

CONTENTS

CONTENTS

PART THREE

PART FOUR

AUTHOR'S NOTE

THIS BOOK IS a work of memoir. I have reconstructed some conversations from memory; others are based on notes and recorded interviews. I relied on court transcripts and legal documents for some sections; in other sections some locations, names, and characteristics of people have been changed.

PROLOGUE

I CAN'T REMEMBER whose idea it was to start taking pictures that night, but it could have come from either one of us. I had a cheap autofocus point-and-shoot, and when Ashley would sleep over, we'd often go through two rolls of film in a weekend.

Sometimes we'd hike into the woods behind my house and pose on rocks or in piles of leaves or standing on logs that had fallen across the river. We'd pretend to be models, trading off with the camera and art-directing an imaginary shoot for *Seventeen*. Other times we'd photograph each other playing the piano in my living room, practicing whatever duet we had learned that week. I was always Secondo and Ashley was Primo, her fingers slender and light on the high keys.

That night after dinner we had nothing special in mind; we just started clicking through exposures at an aimless pace, picking up props we found around my bedroom. There's Ashley, kneeling on my blue shag carpet in baggy stonewashed jeans and a white T-shirt, holding a beach ball next to her shoulder in a mock coquettish pose. There's me, with crazy frizzy hair and Wayfarers, standing in front of a tacked-up watercolor painting we had done in art class.

Whose idea was it to start taking off our clothes? Probably mine, but it wouldn't have made much of a difference. Neither of us was shy, but I was a bit bossier. I wasn't yet even a preteen, but a penchant for directing and managing was already beginning to take hold.

We'd seen each other's bodies plenty of times before, mostly out of curiosity and veiled competitiveness and generally at times when we knew her parents or my parents wouldn't suddenly come home. We discussed which one of us might need a bra first (me) or who looked better in the pale pink culottes we both had (she did).

Sometimes we'd end up in the shower, but never the bath. We didn't look at each other too closely or directly, and we didn't touch; we more just acknowledged each other, as if to say I'm OK, you're OK. We're in this thing—this stage, this girlwoman gawkiness, this whatever it is—together.

The addition of the camera that night gave things a slightly different edge. It was still just the two of us; we pretended to be models, as always, but this time, instead of imitating the glossy-lipped girls in teen magazines, we told ourselves we were the ones in the *Playboys* we found buried in a closet at Ashley's house.

It felt like a game. At the time, sexiness was as foreign a concept as cold fusion. We didn't know enough to feel self-conscious, so instead we just giggled. Unstoppably. We covered our nonexistent breasts with our hands and laughed about how dissimilar our bodies were from the jaded, tanned, and voluptuous women on those pages. We lowered our voices and tried to seduce each other, quoting lines from *The Young and the Restless*, and then we pursed our lips and whistled.

There's me, lying in an S-curve on the carpet, all baby fat and curls.

Ashley, topless with pastel cotton underpants, is hanging from the chin-up bar in my closet doorway, her belly button pulled taut like the slit on a slot machine. There are a few gymnastics poses, then a few mock center-fold shots, and *click-click-click*, the roll was done.

We went to bed smirking that night—Ashley in the trundle below me—with yet another secret between us.

I had nearly forgotten about it until a few weeks later when my mother came home from the film developer, livid. She tossed the envelope of pictures in front of me on the table—unopened—and demanded to know what was on the film.

"The manager came out to tell me, 'We don't develop smut,'" she seethed, hanging on the final "t" as if the word was still ringing in her ears. "I was mortified. If your father had been there, he could have been taken to jail."

My face grew hot. It had never occurred to me that there were actual people developing, considering, and perhaps even discussing my pictures. That it wasn't just an automated machine like the one I got soda out of. That a teenage boy or a middle-aged man or a faceless person I couldn't envision had seen us, maybe even laughed at us—not just this time but all the times. That what Ashley and I did in my room or in her room, or in the woods didn't belong just to us.

It was my first flicker of understanding that part of being a girl meant being looked at, judged, maybe criticized—whether you consented or not—and I didn't like it one bit.

It was 1989, and Ashley and I were ten years old. Today, Ashley is more than sixteen years dead.

PART

ONE

1

FRONT PAGE

SHE WAS FOUND by her roommate in the hallway of their split-level bungalow at 1911 Pinehurst Road in the Hollywood Hills at approximately 9 a.m. and pronounced dead by paramedics at 9:28, February 22, 2001. Her body was faceup on the carpeting near the entrance to their bathroom, and when Jen opened the front door that morning and saw her from across the room, she at first thought it was some sort of practical joke. Ashley was known for her occasional put-ons and tricks, but as Jen got closer, it was impossible to miss all the blood.

It was trailing from Ashley's nose and mouth and matted in her hair. It had drenched the green terry-cloth robe she was wearing as well as the blue tank top that was stretched around her torso and the shorts that were bunched around her thighs. It covered her arms, legs, and hands with a sickening sheen, nearly obscuring the bracelet tattoo she had around her left ankle. It had turned the carpet around her body a dark, angry red.

Jen bolted out the door to her car to call 911, not wanting to remain in the room for another second. She would never spend a night in that house again.

The fire truck was the first to arrive, and then came Detective Thomas Small of the LAPD, Hollywood Division. He noted that the victim was a twenty-two-year-old Caucasian female who was last known to have been alive as of 8:15 p.m. the previous night. He noted that there had been no forced entry into the residence, and no obvious weapons had yet been recovered. He also noted that due to the time lapse, she wasn't a viable candidate for tissue donation.

An external examination of the body revealed forty-seven stab wounds, twelve of which were later deemed fatal. Defense wounds were also observed on her right forearm and hands. Ashley's neck organs had suffered extensive trauma, and her windpipe and right artery had been cut in two. Stab wounds blanketed her back, stomach, and arms, and her head had been partially dislocated from her spinal column.

Bloody shoe prints were noted in the house entryway. The official report from the deputy medical examiner wouldn't be filed for another two weeks, but the manner of death was obvious: homicide.

She was officially identified at approximately 11 p.m. via DOJ fingerprints as Ashley Ellerin, of Los Altos, California. An hour later, a local police sergeant was sent to notify the next of kin: her parents.

It took another five days for the news to reach me.

We sat around the kitchen table, my parents and I, with the paper between us. The story had made the front page of *The Bernardsville News*, below the pictures from the latest hospital benefit and an article on deer population control.

I read it while they stared at me. I was just under two months out of college; in a few weeks I'd turn twenty-two, just as she had been. I had graduated a semester late, and although I still had my same apartment in the city, something about the new stretches of unstructured weekend time unnerved me. How did you fill it all, all by yourself with no essays to write or assigned reading to get done? I had taken to visiting my parents in New Jersey more regularly while I sorted things out. At the end of February there was a bit of snow left on the ground, and my eyes kept settling upon the patches of whiteness outside every few sentences as I read. "Former Peapack Resident Murdered in Los Angeles," the headline shouted. I blinked and knew instantly what was coming.

The article quoted a family friend—someone I had never heard of—who said Ashley had recently transferred from UCLA to the Fashion Institute of Design & Merchandising, and called her "an accomplished pianist and a talented artist." There would be a private funeral in California, the article said. Her remains would be cremated and her ashes scattered in Hawaii, "a place the family had visited frequently and where Miss Ellerin had wanted to live and work."

I felt detached, numb. The time-appearing-to-stop thing you hear about, that was there. The feeling of floating on my back in the middle of a cold lake, staring up at birds chirping in the trees above my head but not being able to hear them—that was there, too. I wondered if my parents expected some sort of emotional display from me and how they'd handle it if I produced one, or if I didn't. Should I cry? Should I drop my head into my hands and wait for my mother to say something? Should I excuse myself? Nothing seemed appropriate, so instead I stayed silent.

I wanted to tell my parents what I knew about Ashley, but I didn't know how. I wanted to tell them the things that would shock them, scare them, and cause them to shake their heads and go silent. I wanted to unburden myself and push them up against the limits of their parental aptitudes. How would they make sense of this one? There was no way to. I felt angry at her, and I wanted them to be as well. How could her life have ended up this way? But maybe it wasn't my place to share what I knew.

They could find out from someone else, or maybe not at all, or perhaps there'd be another occasion to talk about it when things weren't so fresh.

I would wait this time. There were still a million questions yet to be answered. I knew I had secrets about Ashley I was quite certain she had told few others, but I still didn't know what had happened to my oldest friend at the end. So what did I really know, anyway?

2

THE PLEASURE OF
YOUR COMPANY

"I'D LOVE TO," Ashley said when I asked if she wanted to meet for lunch at Pizza Hut on Saturday afternoon. I had earned a certificate at school for two Personal Pan Pizzas for meeting some reading goal in the fourth grade, and I wanted to treat us. I called her on the phone, and it felt like a special occasion, yet I still recognized her choice of words as something a little unusual for a young girl to use, even though I was also one myself.

There was always something a little bit different about Ashley, though, which is part of why the two of us made such a good pair. I first met her right at the time when I was beginning to realize that I didn't quite fit in. The rules of how to succeed at a central New Jersey public elementary school in 1987 were discrete and finite: have the right clothes, be cute and not too loud (if you were a girl), and be good at sports. Despite my best efforts, I came up short in every department.

I had corkscrew curly hair that stuck out in all the wrong places. I wore a combination of Esprit and hand-me-down knits from my mother, resulting in a look that put me somewhere between eccentric and oblivious. I didn't have the requisite CB winter jacket with crumpled lift tickets from ski resorts hanging off the zipper or the Cavaricci jeans with the nipped-in waist and puffed-out thighs. I wasn't a team asset during recess kickball, either; I lacked the quick reaction time, general sportiness, and suspension of disbelief necessary to get excited over who was winning.

My parents worked long hours, and I didn't have a regular after-school babysitter, so most days I stayed in the library until about 6 p.m., when they could pick me up. I tinkered around on the computers, scanned the bookshelves over and over, and sometimes chatted with the other straggler kids, the ones who were in between child-care situations, lived too far out for the bus routes, or had some entirely more complicated—and usually unfortunate—thing going on with their parents: messy divorces, custody issues, restraining orders. It was above my emotional pay grade, but bits and pieces occasionally sank in.

In spite of—or perhaps because of—all that, I acted like a know-it-all: I raised my hand first every chance I got and delighted in winning whatever academic competitions were happening—history quizzes, mock stock trading, young inventors' contests. My older brother—the boy genius, according to my new teachers who had had him six years earlier—was no help, either. He had been an even bigger outcast at our school; after years of being bullied, he had decamped to Phillips Academy in Massachusetts at the age of thirteen to be among his kind, the ones who were doing calculus before they hit puberty and spending their free time huddled around an Apple II. But where was my kind?

I had some friends; some lunches by myself; kissed a boy on the playground who decided he didn't like me the next afternoon. The day I felt most popular was when I found a German porn magazine in my brother's closet and brought it in to homeroom. While our teacher marked papers at her desk in the front, I quietly became the center of something in the back row. The boys flipped pages and the girls tried to suppress giggles, but a few began to slip out. We were caught, and I was marched to the front: scolded—an outlaw.

Baby Jessica McClure had fallen down a well in Midland, Texas, that fall, and we couldn't take our eyes off the nightly news. My parents had a small color television upstairs, and after dinner that week I'd watch with my mother while she ironed the shirts and pillowcases.

I wondered what it felt like to end up in such a dark hole. There must have been bumps and scrapes along the way, and then the bottom came without warning. What did the sky look like from so deep down? Was it just a dot, a faraway abstract thing? I thought about whether Baby Jessica knew what had happened to her and if the fear had ever faded into boredom as she waited.

To me, the images on TV were murky and didn't seem to communicate much; my mother's emotion confused me, the way she would tear up as if on cue. I wondered if perhaps the adults were in on something that I didn't quite understand yet, whether the older I got, the more I'd start to feel.

I liked Ashley right away for a million unquantifiable reasons that, looking back, I can only describe as chemistry and timing. What else was there, really? She had shiny dark hair and a round face, and she didn't rush to try to get in with the popular girls or make too much of the curiosity she aroused by being new at school that year in the fourth grade. Her clothes weren't much better than mine, but she barely seemed to notice or care. Her dad was Jewish, like mine was, which felt like a rare enough thing to have in common that it was meaningful, and we each had a brother, though hers was younger, so she was easily in control of their dynamic. In her house, she was the lead pony for how childhood was going to go down, which was the opposite of how it was for me.

She handled being the new girl much more fluidly than I had two years earlier. New kids always seemed to show up late their first day; I had arrived in the middle of a second-grade spelling bee already in progress. "*Sarrr jent*," I heard the teacher say as the door to my new classroom opened. A tall girl raised her hand.

"S-E-R-G-E-A-N-T," she spelled out confidently, as I stared at the floor while the principal handed papers to my teacher. Who were these kids? How did that girl know there were all those *E*s?

By the third grade, I had sloughed off my newness like an ill-fitting raincoat, and I could stare at the *new* new kids from my comfortable, protected perch in the second row of desks as they nervously interrupted a social studies or math lesson. They always faced perpendicular to the class while the principal and the teacher conversed over their heads, their fear palpable, not knowing what would happen next. Wondering if things would be better here or if they'd still get made fun of for their lazy eye or occasional lisp. I looked at them with curiosity and a kind of empathy. I would sometimes try to imagine the things that would need to happen to have this person end up being my friend. Perhaps I'd be assigned to take her to her locker, or I'd feel a dose of boldness at lunch and invite her to come sit at my table. Their pasts always seemed intriguingly foreign to me—Pittsburgh, Ontario, a military base in Virginia—though I vaguely understood that they had probably come from somewhere they hadn't wanted to leave.

For Ashley, that place was California. It was a place I had never been, but I would end up learning a lot about it from her over the years. Her family had lived in an upscale Bay Area suburb with parks and pools and a walkable downtown where you could get your fruit from the local farm. Her life out there was beginning to feel fun, too: She liked school, she had a best friend, Kelly, and a new cat she named C.C., for California cat. But her dad had gotten a new job—a great job—heading up the classifieds department at *The Village Voice* in New York. Moving felt like a tearing away, a little sour taste of adulthood where things happened that were beyond your control and uprooted everything; things that divided your life into a before and after.

In New Jersey, the Ellerins settled into a pretty, Colonial-style at the top of a hill in Peapack-Gladstone, a horsey town with woods and lawns and a little Main Street where commuters picked up their coffee on the way to the train into New York. They had a white picket fence and red shutters, plus a big American flag out front. At the bottom of the street, there's a graveyard. It's a scrappy, half-moon patch of brown grass with just a handful of graves from the 1800s dotting the centerline. Some are partially toppled against each other and stained with age, others are covered in lichens and mold, all look long since visited.

The families buried there are the ones who first settled in the state in the 1700s, the ones whose names appear on the street signs and park placards: Jerolaman, Whiteneck, Vanderveer. The epitaphs are quaint and succinct: "Our Mother, Ann V., died June 17, 1844, in the 46th year of her age"; "Our Father, died January 1, 1852, at age 83."

I don't remember noticing this place until much, much later, though when we were in the fourth grade, Ashley's mother drove us up this hill nearly every day after school. Back then I didn't know much of death and loss, and I likely looked right past the open field to the houses on the other side, the train tracks behind, and the trees above that. The corner was simply where we turned when we were almost home.

We sat across from each other that afternoon at Pizza Hut, taking small bites from our Personal Pan Pizzas, hers pepperoni, mine extra cheese. It was unusual for us to be at a restaurant by ourselves—our mothers had dropped us off—and in retrospect, the energy felt like a date. Looking back, it may actually have been the first date I had ever been on, even though for most of my life I attributed that milestone to the time I saw

Far and Away with Matt from the local boys' school a few years later in the eighth grade. I was so nervous on the way to the movie theater I had to have my mother pull over so I could throw up.

But with Ashley, it was different. I wasn't nervous at all—I was thrilled. It was finally happening! It was all finally making sense. Though that kind of instant connection was a first for me, it seemed to be exactly the thing that happened when you found a person you loved before you knew enough to think about how it looked or widening your circle or what might unfold if things didn't work out. You grabbed on fast and sequestered yourself and forgot everything that came before. And really, what had gone before, for me, felt like not all that much. It was like an extended period of the TV getting fuzzy reception; you got used to watching your favorite shows that way because you had only a vague idea that they could look any better, when suddenly, someone came along and hit the side of the set just so and everything snapped into Technicolor sharpness.

We were a little too young for those Best Friends Forever brokenheart necklaces, but if they had been around then I would have given her one that day, right there hidden in her Personal Pan Pizza; she'd have to wipe off the oil when she pulled it out of the stretchy mozzarella before she put it on.

Ashley had invited me over after school early on sometime during her first few weeks in town, even before she'd had time to suss out where she—and I—stood, and ever since then there had been no one I was more excited to spend time with. She had a confidence about her that I had never seen before, though from my perspective at the time it looked simply like she knew how to have fun. She enjoyed life in ways I didn't know how to yet—she could laugh at herself, loudly and often, and not be afraid of befriending someone like me. I wanted to learn from her.

We went from being strangers to sharing clothes, food, and dreams in a matter of weeks. The first time we decided to wear matching outfits, it was black stirrup pants, a plain white sweatshirt, red socks, and black sneakers, midway into the fall of fourth grade. We discussed it on the phone the night before, weighing the merits of all the different articles of clothing we had in common and what could be combined with what. It was exciting to show up for school the next day and watch our teachers and other kids make the connection, both of us beaming as heads moved from one of us to the other. We were displaying our link to each other for everyone to see, like wedding bands. We were proud to be a pair—attached, mutually defined, without an ounce of the competitiveness, the "Who wore it best?" that would come to infect later years.

For our first piano recital, we chose dresses that were the lightest shade of pink. Mine was cotton and hers was silk, but when we sat side by side on the bench to play our duet from a book called *The Pleasure of Your Company*, the colors matched perfectly.

Later on, we graduated to just matching color palettes, not always actual clothes. For the first day of fifth grade—picture day—we agreed upon red and black. Ashley went with solid colors, a slouchy red sweater with a black collared shirt underneath and black pants, and I chose a matching Esprit knit skirt and top with skinny horizontal red and black stripes. I wore black tights with red scrunchy socks over them. It felt like one of the most confident days of my life. We had spent the summer together playing tennis, getting lost in the woods, baking cookies that turned out too salty. We brought that with us returning to school that year and wore it like armor. The smiles on our faces in those pictures, both of our heads tilted just so to the left that our jawlines looked almost parallel. Had we planned that, or was our body language that mirrored already?

I spent nearly as much time at Ashley's house during middle school as I did in my own. I can still picture the shed on the property that had a wall full of mysterious neon graffiti painted by the previous owner, but there was also the afternoon her dad yelled aggressively at their new puppy, who had peed on the floor, and the fear I felt watching the way his hand gripped the scruff of its neck. There were the brambly woods we explored beyond her yard and the crumbling abandoned house we found in the middle of it all, beer cans and cigarette butts strewn about the creaking floorboards, glimpses at a potential future of illicit hangouts we'd one day get to experience. High school, we knew, would be the time for sneaking around under the cover of night and adolescence and maybe bringing a boy, or many boys, to this place. But not now, not then. None of it appealed and or even made much sense. What were boys even for, anyway? Marriage and kids and things that were far beyond us. We had everything we needed with just us two.

We spent time with other girls, occasionally, even trying it as a trio for part of our fifth grade year with a new girl named Jill. There were hangouts and a few adventures, but the triangle dynamic never quite took. Ashley and I couldn't help that we had more secrets, more sleepovers, and more affection between us to leave any substantial room for anyone else.

Her house was so different from my own house, where everyone was busy and distracted, and I was often alone. At Ashley's house, people knew each other's business and you could always hear voices through the walls, or piano music coming from downstairs. Bandages were in the cabinet under the sink upstairs, but also one time we found Ashley's mother's sanitary belt in the bathroom, and were dumbfounded. We had been learning about periods in health class, so we knew what one was, but it still felt incredibly foreign and strange. You could use a tampon or a pad, or there was this third option where you hooked a pad between your legs to a belt you wore around your waist. And then perhaps you didn't have to wear underwear? We were confused. It felt antiquated and sexual at once—over our heads.

Her parents, too, were a different sort. Younger than mine, with her dad even younger than her mom. They both were slender with dark hair and seemed almost like TV parents. They would bicker without concern for who was around, or yell at Ashley or her brother in front of me. I saw the both of them more as actual people—human, fallible, loving—much sooner than I did any other adults at the time.

There were after-school art classes—I made splatter-painted abstracts and Ashley, finely drawn portraits of her cat—and hikes and too many overnights to count; the memories bunch together in one long movie montage. Here are two little girls who start out on two adjacent swings, shy, pumping their legs forward and back, swinging in parallel. And then they accidentally bump into each other, and the music swells, and then they're running up the hill, laughing and giggling under the covers with a flashlight and sharing an ice cream sundae at a diner. At the end of two minutes, they are not very much older—they may have different haircuts, or perhaps one has gotten a little taller—but they are clearly, indelibly bonded for life.

There were many years of that. The feeling where we were always each other's first. Where we were partners and pseudosisters, especially since neither of us had a real sister of our own. The year when we devised new ways to pass notes in class by hiding scraps of paper in a tiny compartment in our jumbo pens and then exchanging pens, because it was *that* important that we share absolutely all of our thoughts with each other, even if it was the middle of social studies. The one where we memorized every article of clothing the other had, and as soon as there was a new addition for one of us, the other one registered it immediately. The one where we began to be regarded as a unit to our classmates, that it was known that neither of us would go anywhere without the other. There was no need for autonomy, because we had found the one thing we valued more.

3

THE LAST WEEKEND

THE SCENE ALWAYS opens on that wall. There were things that came before and things that came after, but when the playback begins in my mind, the camera pans down from a long tracking shot that starts over the water or sometimes at the Twin Towers and then heads uptown, moving over Union Square, over the Empire State Building, up the park past the café where I bartended, past the brownstone where I lost my virginity on a random Tuesday in July, down on top of St. John the Divine, and around the corner to that place on 109th and Amsterdam. There were no windows, and I never knew what went on inside the building, but I guessed it was an electrical substation of sorts, massive and looming from the outside, all marble and curious panels of circular, helixlike grating, the shapes folding back and over themselves like sixties wallpaper.

I can still picture Ashley against that mysterious, windowless wall, framed like a photograph I'll never have: her bleached blond hair spiked up with a million little rubber bands, her head turned to me in front of all those steel circles while we walked to my apartment. She was wearing a black, cap-sleeved T-shirt, a skirt with a Hawaiian print, and flip-flops; her round shoulders and tanned upper arms swished back and forth down the sidewalk across from the low-rise buildings and guys hanging at the corner on the block where I lived.

We hadn't seen each other in what must have been three years, that gap between the end of high school and the middle of college when most of my other teenage friendships—the ones that had once seemed a fixture, essential even—had slowly become obsolete. They appeared to connect only with outdated versions of myself that I no longer wanted: the frizzy hair and attempts at conformity, the ill-fitting clothes and the awkward rejections by equally awkward boys. Now I had relationships with people who had known me only from age eighteen on—the adult world!—and I felt liberated: the me with liquid eyeliner and my own place where I could give people a beer from the six-pack in my own fridge. The me who rode subways and played Springsteen on an acoustic guitar. Those former selves, though only a few years behind me, now seemed as far away as New York was from Los Angeles, where Ashley now lived.

We had lost touch, as had happened with so many other people so many times before. How exactly had it happened? Gradually, then suddenly, but also in fits and starts, confusions and forgotten birthdays, faded memories and rituals. The scales tipping toward more important moments lived among other people in other places in other rooms far away from each other.

The Ellerins moved back to California in 1993, during our sophomore year of high school. Ashley's leaving didn't hit me as hard as it might have, since I myself had already left—for a girls' school in the next town and then for boarding school in New Hampshire.

Friendship had gotten easier in the years since meeting Ashley, because I finally had a good model for what it could look like. Our relationship had given me my first sense memory for belonging, and with it came a newfound impulse to seek connection whenever I went to a new place. Starting out somewhere would always come with an adjustment period—a lonely period—but after a while, I knew if I stayed open I could always find my people.

So why did I leave my family and my best friend and a comfortable life that made me happy? Because I held the misguided assumption, at age thirteen, that things could only get better. That I could take my burgeoning self-confidence, newly straightened hair, a new boyfriend, good grades, and plenty of friends and move on to what I knew would only be greener pastures. Tragedy, self-doubt, and regret would never touch me, I was sure of it.

I had surprised everyone (specifically, my parents) by being accepted into a school so competitive, so lofty, that my own wunderkind brother had been rejected from it years before. It was the highest form of validation my young brain knew at the time, and it clearly meant that I was bound for greatness. In reality, it would take me years—more than a decade, even—to get back to that same sense of optimism I'd had before I left.

Everything was different at Exeter. I was no longer part of the smart crowd; I was merely getting by in the bottom half of my class, while kids around me had learned five languages or dug ditches to bring water to rural villages in Africa on their summer break. Making friends ended up being trickier than I had imagined at first. I spent my sophomore fall largely by myself or with another new girl from my dorm whose only goal in life seemed to be getting into Harvard. She was painfully shy and had never kissed a boy and showed no inclination toward changing that fact. I once rather wickedly asked her if she'd consider sleeping with a college admissions officer if he told her he thought it would help her chances. She said she'd consider it.

Boys, too, were a problem. After the spike of new-girl notoriety subsided, I was left with nothing close to the sweet, consistent relationship I had left behind in New Jersey with my ninth-grade boyfriend. The next three years would be ones of confusion, otherness, and the lingering sense that I might have made a bad, irrevocable life decision. Leaving would mean accepting defeat or that I was someone who couldn't cut it, and the emotional sunk costs only mounted with each passing trimester.

Visiting my old friends from girls' school at home wasn't a solace, either. They were happy to see me, sure, but they had moved on in big and small ways that I couldn't relate to. They were getting their driver's licenses and spending weekends at all-night pool parties, while I was forced to check in to my dorm at 8 p.m. nightly and was prohibited to have a car or ride in anyone else's. The kids back home were dating and coasting through AP classes while I was on probation for failing a surprise spot check of my room and had been moved back three levels in French. And they could wear what they wanted! At Exeter, the conservative dress code combined with the New Hampshire winters seemed expressly designed to make the girls look as frumpy as possible.

Meanwhile, Ashley had broken out ahead of the pack by sophomore year in every way that mattered. I had heard she used her grandparents' out-of-state address to get a learner's permit earlier than anyone else around and coasted through the streets of Peapack in their beat-up vintage Mercedes, blasting the Grateful Dead on the radio regardless of what music was cool at the time. She seemed to have breezed through what was typically the awkward period, too, emerging into her middle teen years with clear skin, a compact body, and perfect eyebrows, thanks to pilfered diet pills and the electrolysis she had convinced her mom to get her.

Teenage boys didn't seem to know what to make of her. She attracted plenty of attention from the older ones, the younger ones, and all the ones in between. She thrived off it and the feeling of being in control of an area that the others girls struggled in, while still maintaining her reputation as a relatively good girl. Most of that voodoo I only caught glimpses of during the holidays and the one time I saw Ashley in California during our junior or senior year of high school while I was accompanying my dad to a physics conference in San Francisco after she had moved.

She had driven into the city from her parents' house in Los Altos by herself in a stick-shift Volkswagen beetle. The way she could start on those hills . . . How fearless she seemed!—even my dad was impressed. She took us to lunch at some place near the hotel where my dad and I were staying, and though I can't remember much of the meal or what we did after, I do remember how happy she was to see me. She was giddy almost, like "Look at the caper we've pulled off staying friends this long across this much distance."

At the time I didn't realize how much I might have mattered to her—it seemed impossible that someone as confident as she was would need anyone in her life at all—but I know more now. Much more than I ever thought I would.

I was happy to see her, too, but it felt more complicated. I had heard stories from our mutual friends back in New Jersey about Ashley had been up to, and they made me wary. Wait, she tried *what* drug? And, like, she felt okay about hooking up with a guy that much older? How did that even work? The physical distance, however, and the fact that I wasn't around to see any of it, compartmentalized things in my mind. That stuff might go on, I would think, but that wasn't the *real* Ashley. I couldn't quite picture or relate to what she was doing offstage, so it didn't quite feel relevant to me or to us.

What I did pick up on, however, was the feeling I had about myself the few times we were together during those years. It had changed. As nine-year-olds Ashley and I had been an offbeat pair. We'd talked alike, dressed alike, and crafted our own hair accessories out of Koosh balls and Trivial Pursuit pieces. We'd both been picked last for kickball but had usually managed to stay on the same team and laugh about it. I might have gotten better grades, but the real dividing factors, the social signifiers—drugs, sex, male attention—were still years ahead of us. So were the other intangibles that amplify self-consciousness in girls, the little things that twist the way you look at a friend's choices—and really, they could hardly be called choices at that age—into a tacit judgment on your own.

At sixteen, they were front and center, and with them came a sense of not measuring up. Ashley's body was lithe and angular, and the clothes she wore showed the beginnings of a unique personal style that I hadn't myself yet developed. I was utterly average and had gained ten pounds my first year away from home, which upped the self-consciousness I felt about putting on a bathing suit when Ashley wanted to swim in her grandmother's pool during one of my visits home our sophomore year. Ashley talked about bands I had never heard of and of taking acid at their concerts. I had smoked pot once but was still unclear about whether or not I had conclusively inhaled. And the boys! She reiterated the gossip I had heard, but in a self-deprecating, nonchalant way. She dropped names of kids I didn't know and would never meet. Boys who had dumped their girlfriends for Ashley or tried to talk her into having threesomes. She generally seemed to consider them all rather inconsequential. I was by no means a prude, but my stories of pajama parties in an all-girls dorm and my one botched attempt at oral sex were of no comparison.

Perhaps at the time it might have seemed that we were just out of touch. That, given a few more days spent together, the disconnect I felt could likely have thawed. Instead, I recognize now that something far more crucial was happening: we were beginning to communicate in two different languages, with distinctly different perceptions of how the world worked. Ashley's was the language of youth, risk, and sexual possibility. And mine was—what, exactly? I didn't quite know, except that my sense of self felt defined by limits and lacks, by the things I wanted to be but couldn't, and by the ways I wished the world saw me but didn't.

I knew that there was a difference between the way things really were and the way one saw them, though, enough at least to have an adolescent understanding that I couldn't claim to know for sure how Ashley felt inside, despite thinking that I had it all figured out just by looking at her. Somewhere along our twinned paths, however, I began to define myself in relation to her. Involuntary, illogical—it is something I may never stop doing.

Later in life, a friend in recovery turned me on to the valuable maxim often batted around in AA meetings: "Don't compare your insides to someone else's outsides." That's an exceedingly tricky stance to maintain as an adult; as a teenager, it was nearly impossible, considering that I didn't even have the vocabulary to describe what was happening in the first place. And especially as a young woman, when it was starting to feel like your outsides were what most of the world judged you on anyway. Why bother fighting it?

Somewhere between our fifth-grade picture day and riding in cars without our parents, it seemed to me that Ashley and I had become two sides of the same coin. The feeling didn't start when my mom got those photos back from the developer, but that's the first time I became aware of one of the big forces that would go on to come between us as we grew up. It would be years into my career in media before I'd be able to give it a name, but all along, I felt it like a colorless, odorless, corrupting gas: the male gaze.

It meant attention was on you, at all times, for what you wore and how you looked and whether the proportions of your body measured up to whatever standard was the norm that year. It meant that if you were deemed worthy, a new ocean of power and opportunity opened up to you, and if you were lucky and smart, you'd surf that wave for as long as you could stay on.

It was as if Ashley had taken that essential truth I woke up to at ten—that the male gaze was a given—and stared squarely, defiantly right back at it, while I was still attempting to avoid eye contact for as long as possible.

It's hard to recall if it had started to hurt yet. Most likely I still felt that it was just a phase, that there would be more time, more opportunities, a stage where we'd live closer to each other again. In the years after that, of course, she had called, written, whatever she did or we did every now and again but used to do more of. I usually responded, but I might not have one time or another; the whens and hows didn't seem to matter as much as the vague notion that the chance was always there.

By twenty, I had turned even more inward. I was living in a dingy one-bedroom near Columbia University. Poor grades from boarding school had left me with no college acceptances a couple years prior, so I had begun taking classes in the city part-time and trying for a do-over. Since I wasn't a degree candidate, the dorms weren't open to me. I lived alone a few blocks from campus, scratching at the edges of university life and wondering if and when I'd get the real thing.

I had moved to New York City the day Princess Diana's death hit the news, and at times it felt as though the aftershocks of that crash were still with me. For the week it took for my new furniture to arrive and the cable to get hooked up at the apartment I had found off a sign at a bus stop, I sat on the floor in the empty front room watching fuzzy images on television about that tunnel, that car, that bodyguard, that poor, poor, mistreated woman.

It was the wedding footage I remember the most, the pictures that seemed to cycle on repeat every four minutes on every channel, on and on through the nights. The billowy fabric of Diana's dress and veil, the train that stretched on for yards, the carriages and attendants and those dozens of steps. The whole thing seemed to carry the weight of being choreographed for the postcards and the history books and the commemorative coffee-table albums, even as it was all unfolding in real time. It was as if to make us believe, even just for a day, that nothing bad could ever spring from a scene that looked that perfect. That somehow, if every detail was right, it would keep them—and us—safe.

My apartment was a first-floor railroad flat with bars on the windows and an old radiator that clanged as though someone were hitting it with a baseball bat. The molding looked to have been painted white long ago; now gray chips of plaster and grime pooled in the corners. The floors were linoleum tile made to look like wood, and the bathroom sink was no bigger than a paper plate. Dust collected everywhere, fast and thick, but I soon realized that the lack of natural light made the filmy surfaces easy to ignore.

Despite the dingier aspects of apartment 1W, having people over—something that happened only once in a while—gradually became a point of pride. I knew it was unusual what I was doing—living alone and being alone without being shown how first. No roommate from *Craigslist* (it didn't really exist yet); no older sister who lived a few blocks away to check on me; no resident adviser to field questions or front-desk security guard to field visitors. No one at all, really. I was playacting being an adult without bearing the full brunt of the responsibilities—my parents paid the bulk of my expenses—and when I took a moment to remember that, I realized I was unspeakably lucky. I had my first big party for my nineteenth birthday and served six types of alcohol and played the music loud: Nina Simone and Elvis Costello and the sound track from *The Last Days of Disco*. People danced and kissed, and I felt happy and free. After midnight the upstairs neighbors called the cops, who arrived shuffling down the hallway with smirks on their faces.

My block was mostly four- or five-story tenements, located smack in the center of operations of a drug gang called the Young Talented Children, aka the Yellow Top Crew. Their name referenced the color of the hard plastic lids on the crack vials they sold, which I'd occasionally see crushed into the spaces between the sidewalk squares. Things had calmed down a bit since the mid-nineties, when they had been responsible for eight murders and five million dollars a year in sales, but I always held my breath when walking past the groups of guys on the corner and asked cab drivers to wait until they saw me go inside. Once a homicide detective knocked on my door to ask what I had heard during a shooting that had apparently just taken place on my front steps. I had been watching a movie, unaware of the crime and the buzz of disquieted neighbors.

Mail would sit unopened for weeks, and sometimes a utility or two would be discontinued because I'd forgotten to pay the bill. I tended to avoid doing laundry because I didn't like going down the grimy alley to enter my building's basement laundry room, with LOCK THIS DOOR NOW written in drippy black paint on the inside wall. Filling an empty, full-sized refrigerator seemed daunting, so I often settled on chicken and yellow rice from the take-out place on the corner with the bulletproof glass. One Styrofoam container could usually last me three meals.

I became friends with an obese young Dominican woman who lived upstairs with her two sons and slick, handsome husband. She'd come over from time to time with a harsh joint, and we'd sit in my front room, passing it back and forth, tapping the burnt bits into an ashtray I got from Urban Outfitters.

Johanna never said much about her husband, and I wondered about the two of them as a couple. She always looked harried, disheveled, and preoccupied, the fabric of her pants straining around her hips, her arms weighted down with groceries. She worked a few jobs at a time, often heading to the first one while it was still dark out. Other times she'd yell at her son on the sidewalk, yanking him forward by the hand. Her husband I saw only late at night, usually alone but sometimes with various women with crunchy, styled hair and long fake nails. Dressed in shiny shirts and slim trousers, he'd climb into different cars with reggaeton blaring out the windows. I wanted to believe there could be more to their marriage beneath the surface, but I knew implicitly that things were probably just as they seemed.

One night over a few cigarettes and some cheap red wine, Johanna confessed that her husband had another family in Spanish Harlem. A woman had called her out of the blue one day, saying that their sons were the exact same age: same eyes, same hair, same father. Every time he stayed out late, he was with her, and when Johanna had gone back to Santo Domingo to see relatives last summer, he had spent the whole week over there across town, taking his other son to the park and his other wife out dancing. It was part of the way things went, Johanna said, her voice not even cracking. The same thing had happened to a few of her friends. She had learned to cope, but some times were harder than others. She would gain weight, and then it would get worse, and then she would gain some more. She told me she felt proud to know someone like me, a college girl who was smart and took care of herself. I smiled anxiously and looked at the floor.

Ashley coming to visit was like a strange punctuation mark in a summer filled with more than my usual share of confusion and social possibility. In between a few classes, I had been spending most of my time with two graphic designers who lived together down the block in a medium-sized building with an exquisitely tall doorman. As the year progressed, the doorman would watch me come and go, go and come, mornings and evenings and all the small hours in between—until it abruptly stopped and a new girl took my place. Much later, after everyone in that story was gone from my life, I would run into that man around the neighborhood and we would exchange one of those tight, apprehensive smiles, the kind you might give to your doctor if you happened to see her in the supermarket one morning buying milk. A look that says: you've seen me naked and vulnerable, now move along, please.

The graphic designers were five years older than me and wore suits every day and polished shoes and identical portfolio bags strapped across their chests. I met Nick first, in a philosophy class he was auditing at night that I was taking for credit. Never before and never since have I felt such an overwhelming physical attraction to someone. His blue eyes looked like a mirror image of my own, and I was certain that he could see right through me whenever he glanced over to my side of the room. My face grew hot any time he sat across from me; I took to always having water on hand so that I could sip it whenever my cheeks started to flush and I was unable to look up. Any newfound confidence and self-sufficiency I had picked up living alone the past few years went out the window in front of him. I was utterly, completely infatuated before we had even spoken to each other.

He took me home with him one night after class, and there was his roommate, Oliver, equally attractive and standing at the stove with his collared shirt unbuttoned all the way, half undressed from the workday while making chicken with canned mushroom soup in a small, flimsy skillet. My mind reeled—there were two of them! Men who looked like actual men, who cooked for themselves and had chest hair—I felt as though I were entering an alternate universe.

Their shirts were all the colors of the sun—mustard, brick red, orange—while their ties were dark and their pressed Prada pants crisp and slim-fitting. I could listen to them talk about design until my eyes grew heavy—and I did. How much it all mattered! How animated they could become in their intellectual debates, dense with name-dropping—Foucault, Derrida, Mies van der Rohe—the words rushed out with such intent. How right I felt sitting on their couch, buzzed off all the testosterone and the sense of being that much closer to an adulthood that was most certainly going to be filled with countless scenes just like this one. I was obsessed with both of them: their arrogance, their newness, the way they behaved as if everything and everyone were theirs for the taking—including me.

One I was sleeping with, while with the other I was carrying on a rather ambiguous, boundary-less friendship. Overnights with one; breakfast with the other. Playing guitar for Nick while Oliver sat across the room, rapt and glaring. The guys were competitive with each other, but for most of the summer neither could agree on needing me enough to make me his girlfriend. I alternated between feeling empowered and out of my depth all at once but couldn't stay away either, despite my repeated attempts at trying to distance myself. A few days on my own, and Nick would be at my door, leaving a breathless note or flowers if I didn't answer. But if Oliver went to a party with me that Nick hadn't known about, he'd seethe and pout, his hurt feelings pulling me in like a magnet. Rapid cycles of jealousy, shame, redemption—our three-way relationship had the makings of a Hitchcock noir.

In bed, I was still just getting my bearings. I wasn't completely inexperienced but was nowhere near sexually confident either. Sex felt fun and exciting but also like something I was still too young to understand: its risks, its implications, its potential to be wielded like a weapon. I wanted intimacy, pleasure, power, to be wanted—all of it—but I didn't quite grasp if I had any say in the matter. How did the moving parts fit together? How could I figure out what, exactly, I had to offer and what, exactly, that stuff was worth? What kind of negotiation was necessary, and what sort of language should be used? Was it a barter or more of an even trade?

The things I was used to being validated for—intelligence, talent, eyes—I took for granted and barely even registered compliments about them. The kind of validation I wanted and fantasized about was the kind I hadn't yet heard: that I was magnetic, hot, that someone couldn't stop thinking about wanting to be with me, touch me, fuck me. That I had whatever it was that inspired madness, infatuation, power ballads. I was convinced that this ineffable essence I clearly lacked was the thing standing between me and the romantic relationships I wanted. What it was exactly, I didn't know, but I was sure that it didn't come from being the smart, introspective type, the type guys wanted advice from or talked to for hours about ideas. That kind of thing only got you so far.

Having Ashley inside my apartment that first afternoon was strange. Since the moment I had met her at the train station, she had assumed a quick familiarity with me, and I was still struggling to catch up. Taking stock of her after our long hug hello, I'd had to squint my eyes to register some point of recognition. Ashley was tan, toned, and feral. She wore leggings as pants and had glitter dusted across her temples and collarbones. She talked fast and unself-consciously, moving through the crowd with a physical ease not unlike that of a dancer or a celebrity. Her apparent confidence, the on-ness she had about her, immediately made me feel almost tired in comparison. I thought about the days we had ahead of us, and I felt a vague tension that I couldn't quite place, almost as if I wished I could rewind and tell her no, now wasn't such a great time to visit after all.

We met my mother for lunch at a department store café in Midtown before heading to my place, and I sensed that she found Ashley's tone a bit unnerving. Ashley called my mother by her first name, had an espresso with lemon peel after her meal, and kicked things off with a chatty, rather un–parent-friendly story about being flown down to Cancún by a man who had hired her and a group of girls to promote his new T-shirt line on the beach. She'd mostly worn just the shirts and a bikini the whole time she was there.

Why did I feel as if I had brought home a new boyfriend who was rapidly drinking himself under the table? I took Ashley's unwillingness to play along almost as a personal rebuke. It was hard to find discussion topics we could sustain for longer than a short exchange: school we covered quickly—Ashley was in the process of transferring from UCLA to the Fashion Institute of Design & Merchandising but wasn't sure when that would get sorted out. Family we breezed through, too, as my mother still kept in touch with Ashley's ever since the Ellerins had left New Jersey a few years back, so she was up to date on most of the news. Workwise, Ashley told us about a part-time job she had just taken at Sephora; her boss there was a bit Eurotrash, but the freebies were good. She knew everything there was to know about anticellulite creams. We picked at the remnants of our shared dessert while waiting for the bill, my mother checking her watch often, as was, and still is, her nervous tic.

On the walk from the subway across 110th Street toward my apartment, Ashley told me that the makeup job was just something she held on to so her parents would stay off her back. Actually, she was spending more of her time—and making a lot more money—at a strip club, working bachelor parties and pole dancing for tips; occasionally there were arrangements that happened in hotels, too. She relayed the information with the same casual remove she had used to give the waiter her order at lunch: *The chopped chicken salad, no onions, honey mustard dressing on the side*. So calmly, in fact, that I almost didn't quite register what had been communicated. We passed the building with the little plaque that said George Gershwin wrote *Rhapsody in Blue* there, and I still had contributed only a few words. Inside, the neurons in my brain were sending off electric shocks.

You had to have a manicure and pedicure every week, she was saying, which was kind of a drag, but even a tiny chip in your nail polish could ruin the fantasy. She usually did light colors or French; once she had put baby blue on her toes and it hadn't gone over well. Tanning too—religiously. Men expected you to be a certain way, and attempting to work around that was more trouble than it was worth.

I tried to appear blasé, to take it in stride, but what I really felt was utter confusion. Was I angry at her? Was she telling me this to brag? Should I be wearing my concerned hat now, or would that be unfairly judgmental? Should I just listen and not react? Did she want a reaction? I hadn't yet seen any comparable life developments in a friend and didn't know what it all meant, for either of us or the two of us. I stared at my feet as they advanced down the sidewalk, black sandals one in front of the other. Maybe this was good, cool, right—*To each her own? You go, girl?*—and I was the one with a problem, a prude. Did everything make sense now, or did it all make even less sense than before?

We rounded the corner onto Amsterdam Avenue, and there was the power substation building, blocky and ominous with a few vans parked out front. Ashley's confessions were picking up speed now—actors, crystal meth, the lease to her car being paid for by some guy in his fifties, how much she charged for an hour. She talked of martinis and pills and being on top during sex; the guys always told you they wanted you to go as slow as possible, but she still found ways to get through it quickly. It was almost as if she needed to get everything out before we entered my apartment, an unmasking in public so we could be on the same page in private.

I looked at her face from the right as we walked side by side, her duffel bag shuffling against her hip, eyes squinting in the August sun. Small chin, even nose, lashes blinking thick with mascara—her head fit almost perfectly into one of the circles lining that metal wall.

Ashley wanted to go out that night, and I didn't know where to take her.

She had just turned twenty-one, but I would still be underage for another six months. In her world, I'm sure it meant very little—what with the dates and the limos and all the things that were bought for her—but in mine it did, a lot. I could get alcohol at a few stores and there were a handful of safe college bars I went to, but in reality, my nighttime New York was quite small. The city as a whole felt like a landscape of off-limits places, each one a reminder that I wasn't really as mature as I felt in my head.

I could probably count on one hand the number of times I had been in clubs back then. Even though I had lived on my own for two years, I had somehow missed the memo on where to get a fake ID or project the kind of confidence or sex appeal that got you past bouncers. I had no slinky dresses or four-inch stilettos. Taking a shot of tequila made me gag. I had never done coke—the thought of it scared me. I viewed the girls in my classes whom I knew went out a lot—on dates with older guys, to raves, to sceney Japanese restaurants—as if from across a vast ocean. I couldn't quite decide if they had something I wanted or if they simply had a higher tolerance for discomfort than I did.

From what she had told me earlier that day, I assumed that Ashley had things to which she had become accustomed—velvet ropes, swishy martinis—and that they probably needed to be in place for her to enjoy herself. I pictured her world as one long montage of doors opening, hips undulating, and flashbulbs going off, all with the HOLLYWOOD sign rising up in the background. Contrast that with what I knew—cheap beer, Chinese food, the subway—and I felt a mounting anxiety. My ability to design some epic crazy night out was obviously a referendum on my life, I decided. I needed to show—for both our sakes—that I had knowledge comparable to hers and that I was cool, dynamic, worthy. I had no idea how to do it.

Getting ready for the evening, Ashley paced back and forth from the bathroom to her suitcase splayed open on my bed. She wore nothing but a black thong. She looked outstanding. No one with that kind of body—aspirational, curvy, golden—had ever before been naked in my apartment, stalking the railroad hallway as if in some defiant erotic runway show. I tried not to stare, but I couldn't stop myself. What I felt looking at her: What happened, how did it happen, and can I have some too? Could I have an ass like hers and the jadedness that comes with it, or would the price attached be too much for me to bear?

I wondered what she thought looking at me: curly hair, platform boots, nowhere near comfortable in my own skin. I sometimes stared into my closet—with its racks of cheap denim and cotton T-shirts—and wished for sequins and silk shorts, plus a whole new life and body to go with them. I wondered if Ashley saw her former self in me, the self before she'd woken up—before she'd gotten it. "It" could be so many different things, it seemed: sex appeal, mercenary pride, the way the world worked.

She settled on leggings and a tank top with superhigh heels, and I wore a loose black shift dress and cardigan—the closest I came to a date outfit. We took a taxi downtown to a restaurant that had been impossibly trendy about six months earlier and was now merely buzzing. I had been there once for dinner in June with an earnest guy from my literature class in a halfhearted attempt to make Nick jealous. It was the best I could do, given my limited arsenal. I knew that the place had a basement lounge with futuristic egg chairs and if we got there early we could bypass the doorman. I knew that it looked just trendy enough that it would probably still pass for New York cool to an out-of-towner—even one from LA— but that it wasn't the real thing, so we (I) wouldn't have a problem getting in. Once we were seated, waiters never carded—we could order cocktail after cocktail until things started to blur.

The space was white on white with lots of vinyl and sleek surfaces. There were flickering votives and packed-together tables and a hostess who was probably a model. You could smoke at the bar and on the side of the room closest to the street, so we opted for that part and pulled out our cigarettes the first moment we could. I eyed the corner table where the literature guy and I had sat. That night had been a wash that I remembered with a vague, cringing regret. My date had alternated between nervous and aggressively tone deaf, staring searchingly into my eyes one minute and then, in the middle of our salads, asking me if I had ever considered getting the mole below my lip removed. I had been perplexed and mildly stung but slept with him later anyway.

Conversation between Ashley and me was equally uncomfortable. It was as though the stories of earlier had given a name to the distance between us and now we had nothing left to do but to sit with it. The silence felt like a hole. There were the sounds of the room—forks, heels, legs crossing, laughs—but they were far, far away, as though the space around our table were a bubble of dead air. At one point I accidentally let my eyes grow heavy, staring out the window across Seventh Avenue until my cigarette burned down almost to my fingers. It felt worse than a bad date, where at least then the promise of saying good night and going home alone was ahead.

The things I could think of to say now if I were sitting at that table again, having had more than a decade to prepare.

After getting through half of one dessert—something chocolate—we headed to the lounge for drinks. Descending the narrow back stairway felt like traveling through some dark tunnel of a birth canal. Thumping music grew louder with every step, and I clutched the railing, hazy images of what could be at the bottom spinning in my vodka-addled brain. That moment, that last one before opening the door to a party or a new classroom or a date, always contained a bit of a steeling against the unknown, gathering up the parts of myself I wanted to put forward and holding them tight.

When we emerged from the doorway, things were decidedly moodier than they had been upstairs—darker, charged, a tad illicit. A disaffected DJ was set up in the corner, and there were low tables and clusters of people smoking and trying not to catch your eye as they sized you up. I glanced at Ashley as we headed toward an empty table, expecting to see her more relaxed, smiling, in her element, but she didn't look like any of those things. She appeared blank, rigid, and almost resigned. Perhaps we should have stopped there, gone upstairs, gone somewhere else, gone home. But we didn't.

Cocktails appeared. We stared outward and inward and all around the room, and it didn't take long before the first guy made his approach. He was younger, or maybe older—it didn't much matter, because there would end up being all kinds. They would wear blazers and collared shirts or pullovers and jeans. They would shout over the music, or they would lean in low and whisper. They would crouch awkwardly, or they would pull up a chair. They would have a drink or offer a drink or ask for a light or provide one. Their come-ons would be confident or surprisingly meek, delivered fast and clipped or slow and steady—and they would all be directed squarely at Ashley.

Guys had hit on me at bars or on the street or at parties before, but I had never seen anything like this. The men who talked to Ashley were fearless and stupid at once, and she looked right through them each time. "I'd like to get to know you. . . . I'd like to spend some time with you," they'd say. *Men actually talked like that?* "I felt like I had to come over and meet you. I felt this pull." *What?* How unafraid they were of looking idiotic, how focused on their goal. "Let's get out of here, I know a great place downtown," one said, looking past me as if I were a piece of furniture.

I had never felt more invisible or irrelevant. It was as if I were watching a movie in a dark theater, anonymous and hidden, the action continuing to flicker in front of me whether I was looking at the screen or not. I felt as if I were seeing a portal to another world, one where it was apparently possible—if you were Ashley—to have invitations and affirmations and opportunities laid out in front of you without even having to try. I felt it in my body like a chill, a dizziness. I felt like a creature.

Ashley was cool and removed every time. "No thanks, I'm with my friend tonight." She could get firmer than that, too, when they persisted, turning her head away, tightening her smile. I wanted to ask her how she did it. How certain she could be that none of them were worth her time. Was she even flattered anymore? I would have been. I almost told her that she should just go ahead and do what she wanted, talk to one of them if she thought he was cute, but then I realized it would only make me look naive. Didn't I get it? There was nothing special about this kind of attention—to her.

The next day we went shopping in SoHo. The small boutiques on the side streets and the designer stores on West Broadway and the people and the buses in between. Ashley seemed delighted by all of it. She had loosened up in daylight. She wore black jeans and flip-flops and chatted up store clerks and smiled often. I passively grew sullen to compensate, like a petulant teenager being dragged along by her mother. The emotions that had come up for me the day and night before—the insecurities, the inadequacies, the dark musings—I found impossible to shake off. I resigned myself, for the time being, to the uncomfortable feeling I had while walking next to Ashley on the street. That sense that she and I were operating on two completely different planes and the one I was on was clearly just kidding itself. That we were separate, practically different species and that my form of femininity was somehow lesser. That we were more like distant cousins than present-day friends, our connection was deep and historical and integral to both of us, sure, but we weren't the same. She had the things that made her feel—or appear to feel—in control of her life, and I did not.

She'd be here for only a few more days, I reminded myself, and then she'd leave, and everything could go back to the way it was. At least that—though it wasn't ideal—I knew how to do.

At Steven Alan, Ashley pulled a pair of white cargo pants off the rack to try on, and they slipped over her legs and hips as though they were made for her. How did it feel to have a body that fit perfectly into anything you chose? I had no concept of shopping like that. I felt perpetually confined by the endless workarounds of too-round thighs and upper arms I didn't want to be seen. Those restrictions cut off whole sections of a store's stock before I even got to the dressing room. What was it like to know definitively that if something didn't look good, it was the fault of the clothes, not you?

Dolce & Gabbana lit her up. She wanted to go right in, and I was confused. She had heard of the brand, and she felt adult enough to wear it? She didn't worry that the salespeople wouldn't take her seriously or that they would judge her? I always looked at stores like that—the ones with impossibly thin South American tourists and the $900 dresses—as something that would fit into my life only sometime in the vague and distant future. For Ashley, apparently, that future was now.

At a cheap and trendy shoe store, she bought huge, chunky heels with big Lucite platforms and turquoise straps around the ankles. She thought they were hilarious and would work well onstage, and I couldn't believe it when she wanted to walk out of the store wearing them. To me, they weren't even on the level of fuck-me pumps. They looked like straight-up "I'm a working girl, no doubt about it" shoes. People stared. I tried not to notice. Ashley appeared oblivious to both.

The last stop was some clubwear store by the subway, a place I would never have gone on my own. It was filled with tube tops and loud music with a disco ball overhead. Ashley played with rainbow-colored feather boas and considered a vinyl miniskirt, and I tried to occupy myself with the key chains by the register while she browsed. There was a photo booth in the corner, and we decided we'd give it a go. In we went and pressed ourselves together in front of the mirror, and out spat a strip of four stickers in black and white. Our heads, the size of postage stamps, shone fixed in overanimated smiles. The images told a story: *We are friends*, they said. *We know each other well. We shared things, lots of things, long, long ago.*

Ashley took two, and I kept the others. They've been stuck to the corner of my refrigerator ever since.

I couldn't wait for Nick to meet her. I had told him that she was coming a few weeks before, but now it was a whole new script. She wasn't just an old friend anymore. She was *that* friend, *the* friend. She was the girl with a backstory they wrote movies about, the one with an almost mythic level of sexual energy, confidence—otherness. A girl who would almost certainly never cross our paths in our current insular-academic Morningside Heights lives—though if she did, we'd be talking about it for weeks after. And bizarrely, preposterously, she was connected to *me*.

That idea was both absurd and exciting at the same time, and I even thought it could score me something of a mental double-take from Nick: *This girl is Carolyn's childhood best friend? Didn't see that coming . . .* I had to admit that I was taking more than a little bit of prurient delight in the whole thing. Also, after days of the confusing one-on-one time between Ashley and me, I was emotionally exhausted. I was grateful for any potential dynamic change, even if there were risks involved. I hoped that being around Nick could help reclaim a bit of the confidence I had lost track of, and I was more than curious to see what Ashley would think of him. Those eyes, that cockiness, would they have any effect on her at all, or was that kind of thing just for beginners, like me?

Jump cut. Another cab. This one with the three of us in the backseat. I knew Nick would enjoy being in the middle, so I wordlessly let him climb in after Ashley, who was wearing her new shoes with the clear heels and leggings as pants. I played like I knew what I was doing, like I had a handle on the suggestions I was putting out there. Like I was comfortable with the two of them having their thighs touching as the city lights whizzed past, like I didn't mind if a little tension built. Why would I? Ashley could drop one of her provocative laughs, and Nick could stare at her breasts and ass, none of it was a big deal. It was all free and easy and certainly not threatening—or terrifying—because I was above all that, obviously. Who knew where the night would take us, right? I could hang. The idea that we might all end up in bed together seemed to float in the air—in a fun way!—because that's the kind of thing that could happen when you were twenty (or twenty-one and twenty-five) and good-looking and it was a Saturday night in the summer of 1999. Wasn't it? Sure. Right. Yeah. Let's all have a good time. I could do that, totally.

Even though Ashley was technically the third wheel, from the moment I introduced her to Nick, I felt like the odd one out. He gave her a slow once-over immediately, not even trying to disguise his blatant leering. It was disrespectful to us both, of course, but at the time I only registered the personal slight. I sensed a subtle shift in him that was unfamiliar, almost as though he felt off his game. He'd likely assumed that Ashley would be a girl similar to me, someone younger, whom he could handle and even manipulate if he chose to. Instead, her looks and her attitude made it clear that this was going to be nothing like what he had expected. To get her attention and validation, which he appeared to want—to get along with her at all, really—he'd have to work for it. Part of me liked seeing that, as unpleasant as it all felt. Like, *See, look: it's happening to you, too.*

He made us a drink at his place before we went out, and I saw the way he noticed her moving through his space. I felt young, like a supporting player in my own life. Nick was doing some version of his seductive, turned-on behavior, but it wasn't one I recognized. So many questions he had for her, right away, as if she were immediately this creature of pure fascination. What was her stage name? Prada. How did she like LA? Loved it. At first she was game, even a bit amused. What was her favorite song to dance to? "Black Velvet." But I could tell that after a while it grew tedious. It was as if I were seeing for the first time how men *really* acted around women they were attracted to—like untrained puppies. What was Carolyn like when she was a kid? Exactly the same as she is now. Nick had shown his hand, and Ashley was bored.

Location change. We filed out of the taxi onto an East Village sidewalk. It was late, and we were going to the Tenth Street Lounge. Nick had had the most to drink among us already, and I could see it in the way it took him an extra second to count the bills in his wallet while paying the driver. The bar was a place I had never been to before that Nick had picked. Apparently, he had been with work friends or other women or people I had never heard of at all, when he was off and out being one of the versions of himself that had nothing to do with me.

I was anxious that I wouldn't get in if they were checking IDs, but I felt I couldn't say so. Had that even occurred to Nick? Doubtful. The potential embarrassment I'd feel if I got carded and turned away was almost too much to bear. I had no choice but to wing it, gritting my teeth as we sailed up to the door. I stared straight ahead as if I belonged, following Ashley as she breezed past the bouncer with a nod. For a moment after we'd gone by, I imagined I'd be grabbed by the scruff of my neck and pulled back out, caught trying to pass in a place where I wasn't supposed to be.

There was a long hallway, and then we were inside a packed room with vaulted ceilings and a big diamond-shaped bar in the center. There was a wall with all sorts of recessed ledges covered in flickering votive candles, and bartenders with skimpy tank tops who shook cocktail shakers with purpose, as if they knew they were being watched, because they were. We grabbed stools in the back, somewhere along one of the pointed corners of the bar. We were arranged in a triangle shape, Ashley and I next to each other while Nick faced us both.

I'm the only link between these two people, I realized, and how very strange that is. I had intimacies and an almost primal connection to them both, but their tie to me was the only thing that had brought them there to this very spot at the same time, sipping vodka tonics through skinny black straws. Yet at that moment, it didn't seem to be much of a thread at all.

Ashley leaned back into her seat, surveying the room. Couples nuzzled each other along the banquettes, and groups of girls stood awkwardly in their spaghetti-strap dresses, feet in perfect third position. The guys were everywhere: staring, smiling, trying to catch her attention. I was starting to almost—*almost*—begin to imagine what the world looked like through her eyes. So many men were such a disappointment, clearly. And they all, embarrassingly, fell for the same stupid stuff. You heard the same lines over and over, the same tone, the same way they flattered you and gave away all their power. Couldn't anyone do better? No one knew how to try something different? Just one time, you wished it all wouldn't be so fucking predictable.

Somewhere after midnight, Nick crossed the line. The threshold where, due to drunkenness, arrogance, or perhaps just Ashley's preternatural pull over any and all men, he suddenly dropped all pretenses. He wanted her; there were no two ways about it. And he seemed to be willing to humiliate himself or me or both of us in pursuit of that goal. It appeared as though he had done a little math in his head, calculating a personal cost-benefit analysis of his chances to score with her against the potential loss of our relationship if it happened. He appeared to be going for it.

"Have you ever kissed a girl?" he asked Ashley. Weak. She knew it. I knew it. The bartender knew it, too. I was cemented to my chair, practically dizzy with shame.

Ashley had been asked that before, I was sure of it, by some stupid guy hoping for a little titillation. Hell, I had been asked that, too, but at least one of us probably got paid for it some of the time. Ashley had talked about bachelor parties the day before, how they were easier than being onstage. You just walked in, kept the energy light and buzzy, let them buy you shots. Sometimes they'd want to take the shots off your boobs, and you'd let them if they were being polite. I pictured her laughing, head thrown back, a crowd of men circling her. She was in control of all that roiling testosterone, even while naked to the waist.

I had seen the aftermath of one of those parties before. Once, while staying with a friend's family at a golf resort in San Diego, she and I had gotten into a conversation with some rowdy guys who were out on their balcony in the room above ours. They shouted down and we shouted up and it was a bit madcap and buzzy, palm trees and California bluffs stretching out in front of us for acres. When they invited us up, I felt more like I wanted to *have* done it than to actually *do* it, but up we went. I was on vacation. The guys were drunk, red-faced. There were probably a dozen of them and an open living room with a circle of chairs ringing the perimeter; all the furniture had been pushed to the edges. They told us the strippers had come and gone about an hour ago, and things had gotten a little wild toward the end.

"Wild how?" I asked. They laughed conspiratorially, but no one would say anything more. They gave us some drinks, and then one guy tried to kiss me and I let him while my friend looked on, shocked. I was on vacation!—or something. But really I was on a newfound mission to find out what had happened. Why, exactly? I wasn't sure. There was a spent, morning-after energy to the group, and it felt as though there were some truth waiting to be uncovered. I was fascinated by the suggestion of this behind-closed-doors maleness; I wanted to understand its contours.

"Wild how?" I asked for a second time. Reticence again at first, protectiveness of the guy code perhaps. But little by little, the story came out. I got bits and pieces from different guys, asking leading questions of one and then trading information with another like a seasoned detective. They said there had been two girls and that they had brought some toys that a beefy security guard had carried with him in something that looked like a toolbox. The girls danced with each other in the center of the circle, and then they had pushed the groom-to-be into the ring and traded off giving him lap dances. After that, one of the guys had gotten on his back in the middle, and then they had put a dildo in his mouth, pointing it straight up toward the ceiling. He'd clamped down on it tight with his lips while one girl, the blond one, had sat on his face, moving herself up and down on top of him. The other girl had kneeled over his chest and kept things going, and occasionally the two girls would kiss.

I was floored and instantly disgusted. Did this kind of stuff really go on? Was this fun for them—for anyone? Was this kind of thing a necessary rite of passage that I just didn't understand yet? The revelation seemed to bring an element of danger and extreme raunch to the air that

I hadn't noticed before, but really it had been there all along. I wanted to leave immediately. I grabbed my friend and told her I was bored, but on our way out I asked someone to point out the guy who had been on his back. Laughter again. They wouldn't spill.

Why did I need to know? Perhaps I hoped it was the awkward one in the corner, the guy with a goatee and oversized polo shirt whom I could easily pick out as having something off about him. Only someone with something to prove, or something to hide, would behave that way. It couldn't just be a regular guy or one I'd be attracted to. Those kinds of urges, or judgments, just didn't square. Right? They couldn't. I continued to press, to tease. I needed to make it add up. Finally they told me his name was Dave. Dave! Which one was Dave? *Ha, no way.*

My friend and I made for the exit a few minutes later, but before I got to the door, I turned back to the room, and in a defiant act of I don't know what—indignation?—I looked toward the group of guys sitting near the window. "Hey, Dave!" I shouted loudly, not making eye contact with any one in particular but trying to pass it off as if I had an honest question. Which, technically, I guess I did.

"What?" an unassuming, pasty dude answered. He wasn't the awkward one or the best-looking one. He was somewhere in between, someone eminently average. He looked up at me, more amused than confused. The odd guy I had pegged from before stayed facing the wall, his eyes downcast into his beer. I paused, a little flummoxed, not sure of what to say next.

"Nice to meet you," I replied, while the room exploded into fratty laughter. I turned and walked out, a strange combination of smugness and sadness sticking to my back.

"Would you kiss Carolyn?" Nick said, his eyes a little glassy as some horrendous techno song pumped out of the ceiling speakers.

The night had taken on a surreal quality. This wasn't *actually* my life but some sort of morality play being staged with nonprofessional actors who were my friends, playing themselves, for my benefit. They were here to perform a parable about loyalty, trust, and respect. Perhaps there would be some betrayal thrown in, like in one of those Greek tragedies where only the chorus is left at the end.

I looked at Ashley and thought of Dave in San Diego. I wondered if he remembered that night at all and how that recollection made him feel. Ashley's eye makeup sparkled in the low lighting. She had taken extra time applying glitter over my sink before we went out, and flecks of it had fluttered to the ground and were still lodged in my bathroom tile grout. Lots of other things were sparkling in the room, too. The candles, the ice cubes in people's drinks, the women with tube tops that had bits of sequins stuck on them.

What would I do if she said yes? Was this what was supposed to happen? How gross and strange and possibly fitting. I would do it, I decided, if it came to that. I would take it as something that confused and saddened me in the moment, but later I would look back and understand. It would be a turning point, a definitive before and after.

"I don't do stuff like that for someone else's entertainment," Ashley said, stone-faced. A pause. A long one. "And anyway, Carolyn is my best friend."

Exhale. Silence. Okay, no. Never mind. That was what was supposed to happen.

The rest of the night was in muted tones. The colors were dark grays and washed-out blues, tinged with fuzziness as if seen through some hazy screen. It was 2 a.m. or maybe even 3 a.m. We were back in Nick's apartment. How did we get there? Another cab, another walk across a sidewalk. The key in the lock, the doorman nod. Another key, another lock. A living room. The lights were low. Oliver was there.

He was on the couch drinking a beer from the bottle, still dressed but with his shoes off and his feet on the coffee table. Just back from a date with Katie, a receptionist from work he'd started seeing, Oliver was relaxed and in for the night. He wasn't expecting us but was tired and amused enough to roll with it nonetheless. We were a trio in varying stages of drunkenness carrying with us three very different energies and narratives about the last four hours, but Oliver had entered at the end of act three, and no one was about to bring him up to speed.

Chatting ensued. Ashley appeared to be immediately buoyed by the change of scene and the new player, and Oliver's unassuming bachelor-in-the-wild vibe was working for him. Ashley perched next to him on the side of his chair, her playfulness rising up in a way that hadn't been evident earlier. She was enjoying herself. Even though we had said we'd stop by for only a minute, here she was accepting Oliver's offer of a beer and warmly touching his arm to make a point. Nick glowered. Was she doing it intentionally to spite him? This couldn't be happening. How long was she in town for? What was she up to the next few days? Not fair! It was *he* who had laid the groundwork for all of this, and here was Oliver closing without even having to try. It seemed as though Nick knew it was what he deserved, but that was the part that felt the worst.

It was decided that Ashley and Oliver would go out the following Tuesday, her last night in town before she left to go back to her grandmother's house and then California. I had helped make it happen, as something of a why-the-hell-not as well as a fuck-you to Nick. On our walk back to my place after the night they met, Ashley said he seemed like a nice guy—a good guy. Not like the ones she was used to meeting in LA, and not like Nick, either. We left it at that and went to bed.

The arrangements were made between Oliver and me the next day while Ashley was out of the city visiting her grandmother. I suggested a place called the Screening Room, a retro art house theater in Tribeca where you could order dinner during the show and they served you martinis and truffled popcorn on little café tables. That summer they were showing a series of reissued seventies porn movies in 3D. That week it was *Behind the Green Door*. I had seen the poster on my way to the subway, a backlit Marilyn Chambers with feathered hair and jutting collarbones.

It was clearly a date I would have wanted to be taken on—not Ashley. Part of me must have understood that it would be completely inappropriate for her. At the time, dates for me—before Nick—were made up of straitlaced activities like Holocaust documentaries at Film Forum or dry literary readings in the basement of the campus pub. The idea of something as out there and explicit as watching porn in public—at a dinner theater!—I would have found shocking and ironic. For Ashley, it was a little too on the nose.

From: Oliver Nelson
To: Carolyn Murnick
Subject: before the plane and while awake

. . . i slept with ashley. she is aggressive. katie called in the middle of it. i was kissing to the sound of her voice over the recorder; "i just spoke to nick, he says you're home. i don't understand why you're not picking up." yesterday morning i felt horrid. nick was still being a recluse, and katie didn't even look at me as i passed her in the office (my mind told me she knew). i felt as if i had lost all my friends . . .

And then he continued on about some work drama. Ashley's take was just as unpleasant. "It felt no different than a fucking call," she said crisply when I saw her the morning after. Oliver had dropped her back at my place so we could have a final half day together, but both of us were so tired that we couldn't get up to much. To me, it almost felt beside the point. The hours just flowed into a slightly larger chunk of preparing-to-leave time, which looked like real time only if you viewed it from the outside.

There was a walk to the bagel place, squinting in the sun, and then some aimless browsing in the shops along upper Broadway. Details trickled out, but I wasn't asking too many questions. She told me he had met her at the train, and that he had shoved his tongue down her throat as a greeting. After the movie started, the night began to take on a prickly feeling of inevitability. By the time they got had to his bedroom, she was over it, but figured she'd just give him what he wanted, anyway. It was easier. It was her default. It allowed her to tune out.

I felt intimidated by her casualness with having a one-night stand—was that what it was?—but none of it seemed surprising. Of course *she* was past the point of being affected by the potential fallout from casual sex—it was *I* who wasn't.

I was disappointed in Oliver, too, even though I could see how easily those kinds of disconnects could take shape: the way we pick out a few carelessly observed details about a person and are absolutely sure we know what's what. Oliver was an insecure twenty-five-year-old who saw girls like Ashley as out of his league and then couldn't believe his luck to have her (a stripper!) fall into his lap with no effort. Ashley, on the other hand, for all her experience with men, didn't usually make time with "nice guys" or even ones who were just pretending to be. Oliver, to her, was someone who had met her out of her usual context, her comfort zone, who couldn't afford to buy her much and seemed to want to hear what she had to say for its own sake. She'd thought it might finally be a chance to be herself. They'd both wanted to connect with the side that the other was desperately trying to cast off. I could relate.

We were both hungover, her physically and me emotionally. The party was definitely over. It was time to go.

On the subway to the Port Authority bus terminal, Ashley was chatty, but I wasn't quite there. I half listened to some story about her father, how he was thinking of buying a fat camp and how there was some other drama with her parents. No one seemed to be talking about it directly, so *she'd* finally had to be the one to bring it up her mother, like, wake up, Mom.

Ashley was still next to me on the C train, but already I was taking stock of the aftermath: Nick and I weren't speaking. The girl I'd used to paint pictures and play piano duets with was now a stripper and an escort, and being around her made me feel like shit. She had slept with Oliver after knowing him for only a day. I felt as though my self-esteem were at an all-time low. There was still glitter on my bathroom tile.

The train pulled into her stop. I stood up, and we hugged in the middle of the car, right before she slipped out of the closing doors. Watching her walk away, I felt as if a tornado had blown through my life and turned everything I knew to dust.

4

RIVERS AND ROCKS

I FIGURED I would sort it out at some point: how I felt, what to do about it, where this would leave things with us. Soon I'd feel better about myself, back to normal, perhaps, or just different but okay. Then we could come together again and I'd marvel at how much stronger I'd feel around her. This would be a growth experience of some kind, when I'd look back at it. Later I'd be able to handle everything differently, maybe even have some big Conversations with a capital C. Ashley was Ashley and I was myself, and we could still maybe hang out and not have everything in common anymore and it wouldn't have to feel as if everything were falling apart. At some point, yes, that was how it would work.

She called a few months after her trip, saying how great she thought it all had been and how I needed to come out to Los Angeles as soon as I could. There was lots of fun to be had. For the turn of the millennium, New Year's Eve 1999, she was thinking about going to this big party at LAX, the club in Hollywood. I should come! It would be amazing! I played as if I were considering it, but I knew there was no chance I'd go. Ashley would be perched on some circular banquette in a loud club with a DJ and flashing lights. There'd be disco balls and that thumping bass line that hits you in the gut. I'd be surrounded by people I didn't know in a city far from home. Everything would be too expensive, and I'd be nervous about who would pay. There'd be men all around, maybe even one of those older ones she mentioned, and I wouldn't have a thing to say. One would put his hand on my leg, and I'd stare at his hairy fingers a beat too long. I'd catch myself pretending to laugh and then remember that I didn't belong. Scenes like that could level you if you let yourself get too into your own head, and that was still the space I was in, despite the part of me that wished I could rise above it. I didn't have the perspective, I wasn't far enough away.

The weather had gotten colder, and much of my life had thankfully resolved itself to the way it was before she had come. After a few touchy weeks and some circumspect talks, Nick was back around, and it actually felt as if things might be going somewhere. We were starting a literary magazine about design together, and he had spent Thanksgiving with my family. It all seemed promising but tenuous and, much like my sense of self, held together by a golden ratio of chance and protracted effort. I couldn't risk another potential breakdown.

I'd stay on the East Coast for New Year's Eve, I decided. I couldn't handle Ashley in my world; there was no way I was going to go into hers just a few months later. Next year, maybe . . . or the one after.

The phone rang, the phone rang. I didn't pick it up on the first ring. Or the second. Or the third. Her voice came through on my answering machine while I was lying in bed in the middle of the afternoon, hot and depressed in the summer of 2000. Nick had left me in the spring for a copywriter at his firm, a Danish woman who had broken up her own relationship with her live-in partner to be with him. She'd moved out of her shared apartment into his uptown the same day, and I had taken to coming and going at odd hours to avoid running into the two of them together in the neighborhood.

College was almost over; I would graduate one semester late at the end of the year. I had nothing resembling a real job prospect for afterward or even an idea of what that would look like. I was working nights as the graveyard-shift bartender at a twenty-four-hour French bistro between a few classes that I needed to finish up. I was perpetually exhausted and had gotten used to the buzz of anxiety that had lodged itself in my chest. I had become mostly nocturnal. Drunks and other sad characters I encountered behind the bar occupied most of my waking hours, as well as the per-petually coked-up night manager at the restaurant, who would alternate between hitting on me and ranting about the way I stacked glasses.

Sometimes a woman would come to visit him on her way home from the clubs, usually after 3 a.m., and the two of them would disappear to his basement office for hours. Usually she would emerge by herself later on, but once in a while he'd walk whoever it was to the door. There'd be sloppy giggles, and she would tug on her skirt self-consciously and his shirt would often be inside out. After that he'd often want to chat with me and sometimes share a joint, and I'd feel complicit in something gross. There was a huge glass curtain window fronting the space looking out onto Broadway, and occasionally I'd wonder if some crazy person would one night emerge out of nowhere and slam himself against the thing, shattering it to pieces. Oliver came to visit me a few times, and so did a few people from my classes, but none of it ever felt the fun way I imag-ined it could if I weren't heartbroken, fragile, and half awake.

On one of Oliver's visits, while drinking his fourth Heineken, he let slip a detail about his night with Ashley that I hadn't heard before. Ap-parently while they were at dinner he made a joke that went off the wrong way and Ashley had suddenly turned defensive. "I'm a smart girl," she'd shot back. "Maybe not as smart as Carolyn, but I am." What a weird thing to say, he slurred in the retelling. Why had she suddenly gotten so insecure? Whatever, he shrugged, and then continued playing with the candle in front of him.

A confusion welled up in me, a cognitive dissonance I couldn't articulate. That comparison thing—Ashley had it, too? There were parts of herself that she measured against me and found lacking? I couldn't believe it. There had to be some mistake. Oliver must have misunderstood her. I filed it away as a random one-off as I started wiping down the bar.

"Hey, sweetie! How are you? Oh my god, this actor flew me out to the set in Toronto, so I'm just on a layover on my way back." It was her voice, sounding warm and haughty at the same time. "How's Owen? Austin? What was his name?" Could she really not remember his name? My head was facedown on the pillow. "What else is going on? How's that other guy? Are you still with him?" I looked out the window through the airshaft across to where my answering machine sat on the other side. I listened to her words come out, electronically processed, chirpy. There was a chance to answer . . . there was another one . . . I could get up now, and fling myself around the corner, and grab the phone. I could make it. I could pull it together. Or I could just call back . . . "Anyway, that's about it for me. Call me back!" All right, then. Never mind. I'd get her another time perhaps . . . maybe . . . I didn't know.

Eight months later she was dead and I was reading about it in the paper, trying to convince myself that it didn't matter to me as much as it did. I knew that I had just about let her go in the months leading up to things and it was impossible to know if we would have found our way back together. It would take me years to reconcile that one—complicated grief, I had heard it called. It was what happened when you hadn't cried—at least not yet—and you hadn't gotten depressed, but you still couldn't move on, either. "Why is my needle stuck in childhood?" asked Maurice Sendak. "I guess that's where my heart is." I felt something similar.

It was all the whys and hows that had gotten Ashley from age nine to twenty-two that weighed on me, almost more than the loss. How had we ended up in such different places?

The loss itself left me kind of numb, because part of me felt as if I had already lost her before she died. I had let her go or she had slipped away, off to a place where I couldn't join her: a place of body glitter and body shots, favors from men with agendas, Hollywood, strip clubs.

Maybe because she had seemed almost unrecognizable to me the last time we had been together, it was hard to understand exactly who I was mourning. Was it the girl I had jumped across rivers and rocks with while shouting a made-up language into the summer air? Or was it that tanned, jaded cipher, the not-quite-a-woman who navigated the world using male desire as a compass?

I wasn't an investigator or a lawyer or even Ashley's closest party partner at the time of her death, but I knew there was a lot more to learn about what had happened to my childhood best friend. And I knew that somehow, someday, I needed to learn it.

PART
TWO

5

GERMAN, SPANISH, FRENCH

WHO DID I think did it? Seven years after Ashley died, I still had no idea who'd killed her, and it seemed as if no one else did, either. There had been no news reports and no word from her family, and no one from our town had any information. Depending on the week, I would come up with some vague theories based on whatever movie I had just seen. It *was* Hollywood, right? Ashley's killer must have been one of her clients at the strip club, of course, or someone in the drug world, or maybe both. You do dangerous things, and dangerous stuff can happen to you. Dark shit went down at strip clubs. Mafia stuff, illicit bargaining. Fights and beatings and pacts of secrecy. Ashley must have made some promises in the service of better tips, and there must have been a client or two who took the bait and wasn't too pleased when she wouldn't deliver. One of them had become violently obsessed with her and showed up at her door without warning. Or maybe it was one of those guys' wives who had hired someone—I wouldn't put it past Ashley to inspire the type of jealousy that brought out a kind of madness in people. I manufactured stories both exotic and unseemly. It was all so unfathomable that anything was possible.

It was late 2008, and I was nearly thirty years old. Thirty! When had that happened? I was an adult, people told me, and I guess it did look like that from the outside. I lived in Brooklyn in a large, light-filled loft where I could see the Empire State Building from my window and the Fourth of July fireworks from my roof. I had moved there with an older boyfriend at twenty-five, and when the relationship had run its course, I had inherited a kitchen full of Japanese knives and cast-iron pans to go with my newly discovered domestic side. I had spent my midtwenties moving up the ranks of the New York media world—answering editors' phones at *Interview* giving way to fact-checking at *Food & Wine* progressing to freelance writing and then editing, and then suddenly at twenty-eight I found myself at the magazine I had grown up aspiring toward—*New York*—with the title "Senior Editor" after my name; going to work was a consistent pleasure for the first time in my professional life.

There had been experiences more joyful and wild and decidedly mature than anything I could have imagined for myself when I was younger, but in some ways it still felt as though I was stuck at age twenty. I thought of that last week with Ashley in 1999 all the time, as if it were a parable that I hadn't fully unpacked that contained all the emotional truths I would ever need to know.

I would google her name every month or so, and when I got access to LexisNexis through work, I looked her up there, too. It took a couple of years after her death for anything new to be reported, and it took a lot longer for me to figure out, let alone tell anyone else, why I kept looking.

In the spring of 2004, while I was still at *Interview*, something weird came up. My job had me steeped in celebrity culture—a typical day saw me recording an interview at Cyndi Lauper's apartment and transcribing a tape of Tom Cruise chatting with Will Smith—but suddenly my searches about Ashley brought pages upon pages of celebrity gossip sites. They were in a variety of languages, German, Spanish, French—it was initially hard to make sense of what was the actual news and what was part of the Internet's circular game of telephone.

I finally traced the story back to something originally reported by the celebrity weekly *InTouch*. In the piece, Ashley's family talked to the press for the first time since the murder, revealing anguish and frustration at the lack of movement in the case, and some of it was directed at Ashton Kutcher. Apparently Ashley and Ashton had had some sort of relationship, and they were even supposed to be going out on the night of her death.

Ashton wasn't nearly as ubiquitous in 2001, when Ashley died, as he is now, but still this news landed with a bit of reverb. I wasn't entirely shocked, however. I had seen Ashley's power over men firsthand in New York, and I knew that her circle had encompassed plenty of model/actor types. But *that* guy? How did they know each other? What had gone on between them? Did Ashton know her from her "secret life," or was it something more innocent?

I was overwhelmed with questions. It also felt like a dash of cruel irony to see how far Ashton's stock had risen since 2001, while Ashley's had ended on such a jagged edge. It was amazing how much a person's life could progress in seven years, if given the chance.

The issue of *InTouch* was a few weeks off the stands, but I managed to find a copy through a friend who worked in ad sales for the publisher. He left it for me in a manila envelope at the front desk of his office in Midtown, like contraband.

"Ashton Kutcher's TRAGIC NIGHT" read the cover line. Looking at it made me feel annoyed. Poor, poor rich, gorgeous, living celebrity

Ashton. Did any readers actually feel empathy for him? The story in-side was a doozy. I learned that Ashley and Ashton had met through friends, and they were set to attend some Grammy Awards after parties that night. Ashton had arrived at her house around 10 p.m. but had got-ten no answer when he knocked on the door. He went around to the side of the house to try to look through the windows and saw red stains on the carpeting he apparently later told police he thought was spilled red wine. "She was a very special girl," the magazine said Ashton told a reporter at the time of her death.

There were two nearly full-page pictures of Ashton in the three-page story and three smaller ones of Ashley. There was one where Ashton had stubble and an unbuttoned collared shirt; the other was a cleaner-cut image where he wore a suit and smiled with teeth. "Ashton, pictured at a New York fashion show exactly one week before Ashley's brutal mur-der" read the caption. I imagined some preteen girl somewhere in middle America cutting out the pictures to tack them up on her bedroom wall, the border of the page with Ashley's face falling to the floor.

How odd to see Ashley reduced to a footnote to someone else's mete-oric rise. She was not the story people cared about here; to this magazine's audience, she existed only in reference to Ashton, a sad blip on his bio, his "tragic missed encounter with a beautiful young woman on the night she was murdered." I hated it.

But then again, part of me understood; in my head things had taken on a similar refashioning: in my own search for answers, the story of Ash-ley had also become a story about me. I wasn't just letting her go quietly into the annals of my past. I wasn't just content to remember her and ac-cept the things I couldn't change. I was digging. And grasping. But why?

The Ellerins told the magazine that they had suggested to police that Ashton use his celebrity status to bring attention to the case, but the police had said it wasn't a good idea. "It would have been nice if [Ashton] had contacted us or sent flowers," said Ashley's father. "There is a murderer walking around free," said her mom.

I couldn't begin to imagine her parents' grief. I had written and called them in the first year after her death and gotten no response, and my father had even tried to see Ashley's dad when he was on the West Coast, but the plan never came together. Over time I'd stopped writing and begun to consider my feelings about Ashley to be acutely private ones. There was no one I could talk it over with—our old mutual friends I had long since lost touch with. I filed the *InTouch* issue away with the rest of my clippings in the folder I kept in my desk. The notice of her death from our town newspaper was in there, along with our class pictures from grade school and a few piano music books from childhood. How did it all fit together? Researching Ashley and collecting these scraps of information had become part of my own "secret life." We all had one—that much I knew.

Four years later, everything changed. Finally, in late 2008, one of my Lexis-Nexis searches turned up that incredibly unlikely development I had convinced myself would never happen, the thing I had quit holding out hope for and the thing all the crime shows tell you has only the tiniest chance of coming together after a case has been cold for seven years: a suspect, an arrest, and an indictment. Everything had come alive again.

Details were just coming out: I had a location, an age, and the bare bones of a narrative, like an *Onion* headline. "Area Man, 32." There were allegedly other victims.

He was currently in LA County Jail, awaiting trial and facing the death penalty.

When I read the words for the first time, pixelated lines in black and white on my computer screen at the office, I had to leave the building, go outside. I didn't know where, just that I needed air. I ended up near a parking garage on Thompson Street, my fingers cold and dry as I tried to dial numbers into my phone.

"Something crazy just happened about Ashley's murder," I said to my mother, the story sputtering out in incomplete sentences as I processed it in real time. "There's a guy who lived in her area. It seems like he's a serial killer. There will be a trial and maybe the death penalty. I don't know. Can you believe it?" My head was buzzing. This was my childhood and my adulthood all at once, and I felt I needed my mommy—*a* mommy, some proverbial mommy—to sort it out for me, to provide an order for what this meant and what I was supposed to do with it.

"Oh, honey," was about all my mother said, multiple times, as if I had just come home from the playground with a skinned knee. What else was there to say?

Everything from the past had come rocketing forward into the present and exploded out in front of me in a smoldering heap. My private things—the clippings I had saved in my desk—had become public again, just like all those years ago with the photos of Ashley and me in my childhood bedroom. People were looking now—prosecutors, investigators, maybe strangers, even—they were looking at her and asserting a narrative and claiming it as the last word. Was it the whole truth?

Whatever it was, I sucked it up like my first breaths after being trapped underwater. Finally there was the beginning of some kind of explanation for Ashley's death, and it was bigger and more bizarre than I anything I could have ever imagined. A serial killer? Someone from the neighborhood? This changed everything. All of my pulpy ideas about spurned lovers or escort clients gone violent were out the window. There were other victims involved, a web of brutality I couldn't even conceive of. All of my tacit judgmental speculations about Ashley's drug use or fast crowd were pushed aside. What did I even know anymore? It felt like very little.

Long-simmering, partially formed ideas I had held on to about Ashley and me—did she have life all figured out, or did I?—boiled up to the surface, and suddenly there was a whole new opening in which to sort them out. If this had been a magazine story, the "news hook" or the "why now?" was here, and it would be unfolding across the country whether I chose to follow it or not.

But of course I couldn't leave it alone. I needed to find out as much as I could about what happened at the end, and who Ashley was in the year leading up to her death that I didn't get to see. I knew I would ultimately need to go to Los Angeles and sit in the courtroom as Ashley's trial played out. I needed to listen to judges, lawyers, and witnesses talk about the girl I'd once considered an extension of myself and see if I still recognized her.

Maybe after all of that went down I'd have that exceedingly valuable thing called closure, that cheesy, floaty concept that up until this point I had associated only with romantic breakups. But maybe there was a deeper version of it, too? I felt mystified, inspired, terrified, pushed forward by something I couldn't yet explain. And the real part of my journey hadn't even started yet.

6

210 GRAMS

I STARTED BY getting her coroner's report FedExed to me overnight at *New York* magazine. It was a bit of an ordeal, involving a bunch of phone calls, back-and-forths, and painstakingly worded requests to various county offices. I nearly gave up a couple of times, but then after a few hours or days, or however long I tried to put it aside, something within me wouldn't let it drop. At first I was shown only an abridged version and made to think that that was it, just a tiny dispatch emailed by the chief coroner of LA County, whose signature line included a curious, slightly misquoted line from E. B. White: "People are more touchy about being thought silly than they are about being thought unjust."

What did that mean? And why would a coroner connect with that idea? The guy dealt in death all day. Did people actually find him silly? Did he wish they did? Was his job a constant battle to not lose faith in humanity? This was the first coroner I had ever interacted with, and it seemed to make a strange sort of sense that he'd have some quirks. I had interviewed a forensic scientist for a story a few years earlier, and she had been intense and pointed. I pictured this guy with a shaved head and silver wire-rimmed glasses, wearing a white lab coat and having an exacting, somber demeanor. He'd move into and out of chilled morgues and operating theaters and eat the same lunch every day: tuna salad on wheat with just a thin layer of Dijon.

What preceded the quote was Ashley's life, reduced to just a few lines:

From: LA County Coroner

To: Carolyn Murnick

Subject: Ashley Ellerin

Name: ELLERIN, Ashley Lauren, age 22, DOB 07/16/1978, LKA:
   Hollywood Hills, CA

DOD: 02/22/2001 at 0928 hours

COD: Sharp Force Trauma

How Injury Occurred: Assault

Manner: Homicide

Date of birth. Date of death. Cause of death. No mention of anything that came in between.

I sometimes noticed women who reminded me of Ashley, and sometimes they'd just be girls. Was Ashley twenty-two, the age she was when she died? Or was she twenty-one, the age she was when I last saw her? Or was she thirty, like me? I had to remind myself frequently that she hadn't grown up along with me. She wasn't across the country in the same stage of life that I was. She hadn't actually gotten older. Or changed. Wherever she was, she'd probably look closer to the last-night's-party-style hipster kids with skinny thighs and smudged eye makeup whom I passed on Bedford Avenue while biking to work, rather than me: a woman (!) in heels going to a full-time job in the other direction. But that didn't exactly make sense, because it was now 2009 and she was still in 2001, and I didn't live in Brooklyn in 2001, and the hipsters—who weren't even called that yet—had looked different back then.

It was easier just to think of her as here, though. Now. Back. In the same time period and on the same page. To not really dig too hard into the explanation for how we'd gotten from point A to point B. Or even whether or not we'd still be in each other's lives—we just were. She'd be sitting around my dining room table at one of the dinner parties I had in Brooklyn with the rest of my friends, some new, some older, and some people I'd just met. It was the same table my parents had in New Jersey when we were kids, so maybe she'd even remember it.

There would be plenty of wine and tall candles dripping wax, and the time back at Columbia would feel like forever ago, because it was. That part of Ashley's life would be well in her past, and who knows how it would fit in with whoever she had become. Maybe she would have a lot of the same friends she'd had back then, or maybe she'd have totally new ones. Maybe she'd be married to Ashton Kutcher and the two of them would have left Hollywood and bought a farm back in Iowa, where he's from. (That one, I knew, was a long shot.) She might tell a few stories of those days from time to time, or she might keep silent when the conversation edged that way. But she would be vivacious and humble and mellow, and she would be my oldest friend. How incredible it would feel to catch her eye across the table, no longer girls, all of the years and our former selves between us like guests at the party.

I understood there was a version of me that had died along with Ashley back in 2001—the girl coming into her identity alongside her first best friend, whom only Ashley got to see. No one else was around to tell that story. That girl was like a nesting doll inside the woman I had become, but it wasn't until Ashley's death that I'd stopped to consider how things had gotten that way.

Perhaps there was some part of me that hoped learning more about what had happened to Ashley would explain what had happened to me, too. How did who she was at the end connect to who she was at the beginning, when I knew her? In what ways did the person I was now have its roots in who we were together? If I didn't take this chance to try to figure it out, I felt I'd be missing out on some fundamental self-knowledge I might never find my way back to.

The real thing came in a thick cardboard envelope and was waiting for me on my desk when I got into work one cloudy Thursday, two days after the coroner's email. Looking at it made me feel fuzzy. Had the mail room guys noticed the return address? Did they have to copy it down in a log somewhere in case one day someone came asking? What did they think? How long had this been sitting here, and had any of my coworkers seen it?

I wanted to open it right way, but I was scared. I had no concept of what would be inside, except from those scenes in television cop dramas. Would there be pictures? Would they become burned in my brain? The detectives on television who looked at those files were (fake) professionals, inured to it, but I wouldn't be. Sometimes, in the movies, when a family ID'd a corpse or saw a crime scene photo, their bodies would react in spontaneous, unfettered grief. They would vomit instantly or fall to the ground. I had never had any physical reactions to anything that were as dramatic, but I wondered if I just hadn't encountered the right stimulus thus far.

Should I wait until I got home? What was the correct setting for this kind of thing, anyway? I put the envelope aside and tried to answer a few emails. I couldn't concentrate. I sent an instant message to a friend across the office, a former police reporter turned food blogger. I told him it had arrived.

He wrote back immediately: "Awesome! Can I have a copy?"

I didn't know him well enough to say that I wished he could open it first and tell me it was okay, maybe remove a few pages if he needed to or sit by me if I grew faint while we both looked at it. I didn't know him well enough to say I wished I didn't have to be the chick about to open her dead childhood best friend's coroner's report in her cubicle at *New York* magazine. Could he do it instead? Better yet, how about I just give him the original and never look at it at all? To him, it would just be this strange artifact attached to a dead girl in LA he'd never known who was murdered in a brutal way. How crazy and macabre. Like in *The Black Dahlia*. That would be way more interesting to leaf through for a few minutes than writing about bitters and pork buns and whatever else he was being paid to care about.

"Um. Yeah, I guess so" I wrote back. "Will swing by later."

Time to pull it together. I had gotten this far, and it was only the beginning. I got up from my desk and headed to the kitchen to grab some water and then on down the hall to a small interview room where I could lock the door behind me. I pulled the string tab across the FedEx envelope and let the paper curl drop to the floor. There were about fifty white pages inside. Loose. No envelope, no cover letter.

I was slightly light-headed, out of my body. The first page was her toxicology report. There was a lot of white space. I took it in with squinty eyes before I gathered that nothing there would freak me out too badly. Alcohol, barbiturates, cocaine: she tested negative for all. I was surprised.

Wasn't Ashley a party girl? Wasn't her life just one big stretch of VIP rooms and designer drugs? Hell, even *I* had at least a glass of wine most nights. Didn't something like marijuana stay in your system for weeks?

She hadn't had at least one drink waiting for Ashton to pick her up or a bump the night before?

I had felt certain that there would be at least some information in the report, something about her insides that I didn't know, that you couldn't tell just by looking at her. Something tiny that might make me think *Aha* or *Yes, of course*; she'd had all these experiences that I couldn't relate to; I could emotionally distance myself a bit. Wouldn't it all just make sense now? But it didn't. I felt sad in a new way.

What if I had gone to see her that New Year's Eve 2000, as she'd wanted me to, and then the next chapter of our friendship might have begun? What if I had just chilled out and sat next to her at some loud club and been there when the ball dropped and the glitter fell and I watched as she flirted, drank, and laughed? Maybe it wouldn't have been so bad a time after all. Perhaps I would have made out with someone adorable and random or spilled champagne all over my dress, and the next morning I'd still be able to smell it and it would make me smile.

Maybe after that Ashley and I would have gotten a ride from someone cute who was hitting on her and then we would have stopped at some all-night diner and eaten pancakes and grilled cheese and things might have started to seem familiar again. And what if I had visited LA just one time after that, perhaps then the conversations would have started. The late-night ones, after a bit of vodka or wine or maybe pot. Yes, I did enjoy it when I could get it, but I didn't have a hookup or anything. She'd laugh at that, and I wouldn't care. She'd say that she was lonely and I'd say that I was, too, and she'd say that she was angry sometimes and wondered when the real part of life was going to begin. I'd tell her that I wasn't sure Nick would ever love me in the way I wanted him to, and I wouldn't feel afraid at all. I would have wanted to pick up the phone when she called later on, and if I'd missed it I would have dialed back right away. That week in New York had to have happened the way it did, I'd think; it was just something like growing pains between us.

The next section was called "Investigator's Narrative." It was two pages of print with the LA County seals at the top. Single-spaced. The who-what-when-where but not, of course, the why. There would never be a clear answer for the why, I knew, and even if there was, it wouldn't be something that could be typed out succinctly on a keyboard in a musty city office building.

Most of the form was written in a detached first-person voice by a detective named Small. There were also references to a Lieutenant Smith. Such storybook names these people had, they seemed almost made up. The descriptions of the scene and the evidence were vague and brief, as the investigation was still ongoing, it was noted. I could read all those lines numerous times and feel nothing—"No suspect in custody . . . a hair and fingernail kit were collected." Hard-boiled language that I'd heard a million times in voice-over.

The "Body Examination" part was a little more detailed, and that was what started to make my pulse pick up in a queasy way. "Decedent was observed lying in a supine position, leaning toward her left." The use of the word *decedent* paired with the feminine pronoun caught me. "Decedent" was so clinical, like you were just talking about a thing or even an animal, whereas "her" was a person. "Her" was Ashley. Was I reading about an object or a human life, or something else in between?

"She was dressed in a light green bathrobe, a blue tank top, and blue shorts." If you had just seen that sentence, you wouldn't have guessed it was from a coroner's report describing a murder scene. It could have come from anywhere, even a wedding announcement, describing what the bride had worn while getting her hair and makeup done and sipping a flute of champagne. What kind of wedding would Ashley have wanted?

I couldn't remember if it was something we had ever talked about or even if she saw herself eventually in a settled-down life at all. I wondered if the tank top and shorts matched, like was it a cotton camisole set? I typically wore just yoga pants and a bra around the house, but I pictured Ashley in only matching lingerie sets and slips from France or Italy that maybe a man had bought her. This outfit sounded as if it could have been one I might have had, like many-times-washed high school stuff from the Gap.

I drank some water and kept reading. I had been away from my desk for only a few minutes, but I suddenly felt acutely aware of time. "Several stab and cut-type wounds were noted, particularly to the head, neck, the front and back torso, and the left leg. Apparent defense wounds were noted as well." Defense wounds. The phrase gave me chills. The first reference to her body as animated—clawing, desperate, alone. Stabbed in the fucking head. The words made my scalp ache. I didn't know if I could process the rest of the section, to take it in and not just let it skim the surface. Somehow I still felt it was my obligation to properly bear witness to it all—her wounds, her suffering—and to do that I had to picture each and every phrase as it might have happened to her, or to me. "An obvious skull fracture was also observed to the back area of the head." It wasn't just a random skull that was broken like a vase that had fallen off the shelf. I thought of Ashley's head, with shiny hair that used to be brown but then became blond. The amount of force it would take to break a skull. The rage and the animalism of the person who had done this to her. Who was it? Why did he do it? I skipped ahead, vowing to come back later after I had given the entire thing a once-over.

The following page had only a line for the next-of-kin notification, which had occurred around midnight, about an hour after Ashley's identity was confirmed from her fingerprints. The information was redacted; all of the words and the entire address line were obscured, but I could just make out the edges of a few letters at the beginning of the name:

M-I-C-H. I knew what was under there, in the part that the coroner didn't want me to see.

Michael. Ashley's dad.

He picked us up from piano lessons, sometimes dropping us off, too, and later he began staying through the entire hour, sitting on the couch against the wall and writing notes on a narrow reporter's pad. The following year, he started taking lessons himself from our teacher, Ms. V., a young, athletic-looking woman with close-cropped hair who wore overalls and cardigans and had a couple of cats who would wind themselves around the piano legs as we played. I thought it odd that a guy in middle age would be taking piano lessons from his daughter's teacher, spending all that time around her house when he didn't have to. Both the paternal attentiveness and an adult spontaneously coming up with a newfound hobby felt unfamiliar to me.

Years later, when I'd watched my own mother sign up for lessons with Ms. V. at the age of seventy after losing her own mother, I'd come to understand it differently. Adulthood was complex and demanding; aging, irreversible. It was easy to see the appeal of traveling back in time, carving out an hour when your greatest concern could simply be to master the fingering of "Minuet in G."

I stopped reading there, for the time being, and went back to my desk to edit a restaurant review.

For lunch, I walked outside to grab a salad and ate it while sitting on a stoop on West Broadway, just a few doors down from where Ashley had led me into Dolce & Gabbana all those years back. It felt funny and odd and perhaps important that my office, years later, had ended up being just blocks away from some of the locations I most associated with our last week together in New York. There were multiple pins on my emotional map of Manhattan related to her that I now had to pass every day. *New York* magazine's offices were downtown in a formerly industrial section on the waterfront that developers were trying to rebrand as Hudson Square. I now worked in a hulking seventeen-story converted printing building right atop the Holland Tunnel that sat at the intersection of Chinatown, SoHo, and Tribeca. Street vendors hawked fake Fendi bags and blown-glass hookahs along Canal Street, and across the street was the former Screening Room—now called Tribeca Cinemas—the movie theater where Oliver and Ashley had had their seventies porn-in-3D date ten years earlier. I could almost picture them on the sidewalk together like ghosts as I walked to the A train in the evenings. They were playful and buzzed and the night was just beginning, and I saw them holding hands, even though I'm nearly positive that never occurred.

Around the corner was the site of that clubwear store where she and I had ducked into the photo booth and I had tried to feign interest in the glittery hot pants and feather boas that delighted her. The place was empty now, but the facade looked exactly the same, and I'd pass by it on the way to my favorite coffee place on Spring Street and catch my reflection in the glass. The feeling of the area had changed a bit, too, becoming slightly more homogenous and monied. There seemed to be more European tourists around, and, of course, there was no more shadow from the Twin Towers.

In the afternoon, I made a copy of the report and dropped it off with my coworker who had asked for it, even before I had finished reading it myself. "Cool!" he said. I had a fleeting thought that perhaps I should be protective of the thing, that maybe it was a bit unseemly to be sharing it with someone who would take it in like some spooky campfire tale. Whatever. He was interested in his own way, and he was a good guy. I was more worried that I had accidentally left a page in the photocopy machine and someone in the office would find it. I returned to double-check, twice.

I went back to the interview room to read the next section. It was dense and medical, twelve pages cataloguing the external examination of Ashley's body as well as detailed descriptions of her injuries. "There are a total of forty-seven (47) sharp force traumatic injuries including stab wounds and incised wounds. Twelve fatal wounds will be discussed in detail." Forty-seven stab wounds! It was impossible to fathom. As an experiment, I began tapping my left hand against my chest, counting up from one to forty-seven. My arm got tired at around twenty-three. By thirty it felt as if things had gone on forever. After forty I began to feel silly, but I continued to the end.

I could close my eyes and picture a girl in a bathrobe and camisole being knocked down to the carpet and pummeled with a riot of force. There were sounds at first, I could hear them. Cries and tears and then later just his grunts and the sickening whoosh of velocity and tearing flesh. Her body was devastated and mangled. I was viewing it from far away, so I could only really register the energy leaving her. The rising of the chest getting slower and slower. She was unconscious. It was not Ashley. It couldn't be. I tried to picture someone else, someone I had been with more recently, or even myself, and I couldn't do that either. "The soft tissues of the neck have been entirely transected, and this incised wound extends into the right aspect of the cervical spine." I couldn't do it because it was so far out of my frame of reference, so far beyond anything I had ever seen before. I had never been in a war zone. I had never even seen a dead body. I could imagine details from plenty of other things that I hadn't seen happen—the future birth of my first child, hitting a deer with my car—but Ashley's head being nearly severed from her body, her neck completely flayed? No. Sorry.

Wound no. 20 had punctured her spleen and gone approximately six inches deep. Where was your spleen? I made a note to google it when I got back to my desk. Wound no. 26 was to her spine, from the side. Wound no. 27 had gone through Ashley's right lung and was six and a half inches deep. Six inches was longer than the length of my hand. So that meant something had gone that deep straight into her chest from the outside? No. 19 was through the back, but it had also hit the right lung. How was she being stabbed from all sides at once? Was he rolling her over and back again? This was getting too abstract. I was no longer light-headed, no longer dizzy. I was simply numb.

At dinner parties or on a date or in one of those long conversations with someone new where it feels as though you're really showing each other essential parts of yourself or telling your sad stories, I'd begun to practice talking about her in different ways.

"My childhood best friend was murdered at twenty-two," I'd say. *Thank you, yeah, I know. It was a while ago, and we were sort of estranged at the time.*

Or "My friend who was killed, there were some things about her life that were kind of shocking, that she told me about the year before and I didn't know what to do." *Yeah. It's kind of heavy. I still don't really know if I've processed it. It can make me feel like an asshole sometimes.*

Occasionally I'd go a little further at the outset. "Did you ever have a friend who you were really close to as a kid and then you went in different directions and thinking of them felt sort of complicated?" Everyone did. "I'm not sure how it is for guys," I'd say if I was speaking to one, "but to girls, there always seems to be this thread of competitiveness that sneaks into things when boys enter the picture, like one of you has to be the pretty one and the other is the smart one." People seemed to grasp that concept. "But Ashley and me," I'd go on, "we were sort of bonded before all of that started to happen . . ." I'd trail off, feeling self-conscious. "But then . . . well, she represented a lot of things," I'd say, and then look up, searching.

Did I feel guilty that I had let our friendship go? People would always ask, a little sheepishly usually. Time went by, and the answer changed. In the years directly following her death, it was no. I thought of her all the time, but I hadn't really cried. "I was young, too," I'd say. "I didn't know how to start the hard conversations, like asking her if she was happy or felt safe or what she really wanted to do with her life and was this really it? I didn't know what I was supposed to say."

The female friends I had in my life now I loved enthusiastically, sincerely. We showed up for one another—breakups, moves, family funerals—and frustrated one another, but most of all we saw one another, in the truest sense of the word. We bore witness to one another's lives and struggles. We asked one another the tough questions and stuck around for the answers, even if we didn't know what to do with them. I didn't fault myself for not having seen things that way when I was younger, however. It had been a process of trial and error to get to this place.

It was easy to lose people to the tides of New York City, but by the end of my twenties I had figured out who was worth holding on to, and hold on I did. I let my friends know how much they meant to me and felt genuinely invested in their happiness. Most of these people I had known only since after college, though. A few went back to high school, but no one earlier than that. No one went as far back as Ashley would have. Not even close.

Later I found an anthology online called *Headless Man in Topless Bar: Studies of 725 Cases of Strip Club Related Criminal Homicides*, and I read through it in a week. It was telephone-book thick. Ashley wasn't in it, but dozens of other dancers, clients, and escorts were, and many of the cases were unsolved. The fact that the book even existed, and that killings would be grouped together in that way, felt sickeningly cynical. The tone of the book left me cold, as though people saw the murder of women who worked in the sex industry as all the same and that they got what was coming to them for having slipped into this dark and shameful underworld.

But part of me understood that I was trying to make my own sort of calculation. I never once thought that Ashley was to blame for her own death, but I couldn't help wondering about the ways in which her lifestyle might have put her in harm's way. It was a risk assessment we all did, a way to pretend we saw bad things coming after the fact while trying to make sense of the world. *He died of lung cancer, yup, smoked a pack a day . . . It was a mugging, yeah, Bushwick at four in the morning—no good.* Ashley was beautiful and wild and teased men and used them, and danger came knocking. There had to be a connection, right?

Someone, somewhere knew the answer. I'd drive by her old house in Peapack when I went home to visit my parents and park my car at the end of her driveway, sitting for twenty minutes at a stretch without really knowing why. I'd stare at our class pictures and snapshots from concerts and trips, hoping to have some epiphany, though I had no idea what kind. Someday I'd put together exactly what stories I attached to that last week in New York, I'd tell people. I'd figure out what it all meant to me and why it still felt so alive. Someday, yeah, I would do all that.

The final part was the drawings—the location of her wounds marked up on a body diagram with arrows numbering each one that referenced an earlier form. The visual effect was like a game of Operation crossed with the acupuncture posters I'd seen in storefronts in Chinatown. By this point, I had been immersed in the language, the phrases, and the protocol of violence made clinical for the better part of a day. I had read detailed descriptions of the state of each of Ashley's excised, traumatized organs, followed along as the neuropathologist used a Stryker saw to cut a cross section through her brain, and learned that her heart weighed 210 grams. After looking through dozens of pages, I felt as if I had moved from emotional engagement to dissociation again. I was ready for this to be over.

The diagram was a bald, androgynous figure, with the outline of his/

her body from the back and the front splayed out. There were no breasts or genitals; however, the curve of the ass from the back looked decidedly feminine. The wounds on the front of the body, the ones marked "gaping," were drawn in a leaf shape, almost as if this hairless, genital-less naked person had fallen asleep under an elm tree and the wind had blown a few stray leaves down upon her chest.

That evening, at the end of work, I put all the coroner's pages back into the FedEx envelope and slipped the whole thing into my purse. I got on my bike and headed across town to meet my chef friend Dan at a cocktail party. There was aquavit in little crystal glasses, and I drank many. There were tiny canapés such as tuna tartare with smoked salt, and I ate many. There were flirting and toasting and I had almost let the feelings and the images of earlier in the day slip my mind until I reached into my bag for something and felt the hard edges of that envelope.

On nights like these, it was impossible to ignore the guilt question. But even when I wasn't having a rosy, buzzy, fortunate sort of time, I recognized that my perspective had shifted over the years. It wasn't just that it looked as if they had found the guy and that he didn't seem to have had anything to do with Ashley's "secret life." I felt a little guilty that I had assumed that it would all add up. But there were other feelings that were more insidious.

It's a complex thing, guilt. I knew that now, whereas before it used to seem a lot more discrete. I thought you either felt it or you didn't and that it would be obvious which was which. But now—survivor's guilt, bargaining, there were so many different kinds that ebbed and flowed, and when you went looking you could find them everywhere. It would be Ashley's birthday, and I'd wonder if I had said X to her on Y date, maybe she and I would have been closer in her last year. Boom: guilt. But . . . who knows if that had happened, if she still wouldn't be dead today? It would be naive to think that could have changed the outcome. Or I'd be disappointed by someone and think that if Ashley were alive we'd have been friends for more than two decades, and you really don't get too many chances for long relationships like that. I should have valued that more, been around, reconnected, found out what she really wanted from life, and given her my support. Maybe she needed more of that back then. Boom: guilt. But . . . most people don't think like that at age twenty. That's one of the defining features of being twenty, actually.

It was excruciatingly unknowable: why she was her and I was me and she was there and I was here. That was really what guilt felt like to me, I understood now: trying to organize that impossible pile into a shape I could live with. I had been doing it all along.

There were many times when I'd felt just outside the events of my own life, including some of the time I had spent with Ashley. She was someone who jumped in without caring what people thought—sailing down Broadway on heels of chunky Lucite—and now, without intending to, I realized she'd given me a reason to take some pretty bold actions of my own.

I could feel myself picking up speed. I now had the precise outline of the violence and pain Ashley had faced at the end, the terrifying, unfathomable wounds she had suffered, but it still felt like just the beginning. Who was she, really, to the people who knew her and loved her that final year? Who was the killer, and how did they cross paths?

I didn't want to wait for the next judicial proceeding for more information. Though I wasn't quite ready to dive headfirst into Ashley's LA world, I could reach out to someone I already knew to see how it felt as practice, someone I didn't need to be intimidated by. He might not have much to offer me, but in many ways he'd be a perfect test case for helping me to learn about a side of Ashley I had never seen on my own. I would start with Oliver.

7

THE DAY MICHAEL JACKSON DIED

"YOU'RE A LONG way from home," a woman is saying to me, both of us seated in an empty movie theater, waiting for the show to start. It is the summer of 2009, and I'm in Seattle to meet my old friend Oliver and ask him what he remembers about Ashley—only he doesn't know it yet. The anticipation is making me anxious, fidgety, more talkative than normal, and unable to eat more than a few bites.

Seattleites are reasonably friendly, I am finding, so when they ask me where I'm from and what brings me to their city, I tell them the truth. I tell the truth in varying degrees of detail, though, depending on my audience. To the cab driver who picks me up from the airport, a stoner girl with dreads, younger than me, I play up the friendship angle. To the U-Dub professor I meet sitting at the counter of one of Seattle's better tattooed-chef-small-plates spots, I talk more about research and interviewing. To the guy I meet at a wine bar around the corner from the restaurant, I talk about crime and secret lives. He asks me to go to a jazz club with him later that night, and I can tell it's a bolder move than he's used to making. I decline.

Michael Jackson died the day before, just as I was leaving my office at *New York* for JFK. From the time it takes me to get from lower Manhattan to Queens, the news has mutated from "developing" to "nobody in the world anywhere could be caring about anything other than this."

On the flight out west, everyone's seat-back mini-televisions flash the same pictures: crowds up in Harlem; crowds outside the Los Angeles home; the young, hopeful kid in bell-bottoms; the emaciated man at the end. Commentators speak solemnly about Michael's demons, his loose grasp on reality, and the outpouring of public grief not seen since the death of Princess Diana. The cultural footnote seems oddly fitting as a backdrop to what's going on in my head. Something big is happening out there, too.

Oliver and I haven't spoken in almost a decade, not since a short while after that weekend he slept with Ashley, my last weekend with her. My breakup with his roommate had been messy, and I'd told myself I needed to cut all ties.

Oliver did know Ashley was dead, because I'd told him with a melodramatic flourish when I'd run into him on the subway a few months after it happened. "Remember my friend from LA who you fucked when she visited me two summers ago? She was murdered." And then I just about turned on my heel and exited stage left. I took some satisfaction in the shock I got to wield like a weapon. Girls whom you have one-night stands with are people, too, I was trying to say. Their lives continue even if you forget them. They are flawed humans just like you who shit and cry and sometimes end up stabbed to death in their living rooms.

I didn't blame him for being a bit of an aggressive dick on his date with Ashley, though. Not anymore. I had seen enough to understand that most people back then, all of us in our early twenties, really, had never given too much thought to the marks they were leaving on each other—the flake-outs, the fights, the betrayals. No one seemed to remember that there might not be a chance for a do-over, and they certainly weren't making time for one. We were all living in the moment, just like Oprah had taught us to do. We all thought we had but world enough and time to screw up, fuck up, cheat, and mistreat each other and still have it turn out okay in the end. It had to, right?

Oliver comes to meet me in the lobby of the Ace, the trendy boutique hotel where I'm staying for the weekend. He knows I'm in town on some kind of writing assignment, but I've intentionally kept the details vague. I feel a bit like an undercover operative as I walk down the stairs from my room, my stomach and head buzzing, having downed a glass of wine in my room while getting dressed.

I reach the ground floor and there he is, standing three feet in front of me with the six o'clock sunlight coming in through the windows as a backdrop. He looks older, softer, slightly worn down by life. He's dressed like a student, a messenger bag slung across his chest, a rumpled plaid button-down peeking out from beneath an outdoorsy-looking jacket. I can see his recent divorce in the lines around his temples, and he has a bit of a paunch where there was once only stocky muscle. I exhale. I remember this guy.

We lock eyes, and in that moment I see a flash of myself the way he must see me. I'm no longer the insecure twenty-year-old who cried over his narcissistic roommate way back when. I'm not the girl he used to eat ice cream sandwiches with on his tar-covered roof or visit late at night at the crappy French place where I bartended badly. I'm a woman, unmistakably, wearing four-inch heels and a blue silk slip dress, walking toward him to take his hand. Suddenly the night feels full of possibility.

Oliver has an itinerary in mind for us, and he links his arm with mine as we walk toward the waterfront. We get beers at a bar in a converted warehouse with a big back garden, and almost right away we're laughing. There's an excited, flirtatious energy to it all, part of it coming from the realization that we are both now adult, we've given ourselves permission and agency to get what we want. I had forgotten how well I used to get along with him and that he had once told me he loved me on a rainy night while crossing Broadway at 102nd Street. Things feel familiar and new at once, and it occurs to me that the reason I'm here may not be what I thought it was when I got on the plane.

We go to a Japanese place where Oliver says he had dinner with his parents when they visited from Ohio. We're both a little buzzed, and he orders a bottle of wine and barbecued pork belly and lots of meat on skewers. He's telling me how things fell apart with his wife and then admits that he's not sure he ever really wanted to get married. He asks me if I'm seeing anyone back in New York and I'm coy about the answer, but he persists and I continue to demur. I can't put my finger on when things slide into date territory, but at this point we are decidedly there.

His arms are around me now, both of them. We're pressed next to each other on a banquette at Chop Suey, a small, kitschy rock club in the Capitol Hill neighborhood. It's dark; the bar is dimly lit in red with lots of hanging Chinese lanterns, and there's a flashing glare from the band though we're turned away from the stage.

A couple of moments have gone by when I'm close to getting the words out, to telling Oliver the real reason I'm here, with him, in this place. But then I look into his eyes and I see that he wants me and I can't open my mouth. I assume that as soon as I say it, the whole tenor will change, and I'm not sure I'm ready for that. Maybe I can hold off and just relax tonight, I think. Maybe the big stuff can wait until tomorrow.

The music behind us is practically drowning out my thoughts, and Oliver's hand is on my upper thigh. I think he's about to kiss me, and almost despite myself my body tenses and the practiced, sobering line slips out: "I'm here to talk about Ashley."

Oliver's hand stays where it is, his eyes maintain their tipsy, googly-eyed soft focus, and for a second I wonder whether he's heard me.

"Ashley?" he asks, without any recognition.

"My friend Ashley from LA. The one you slept with who was murdered."

"Ah. Okay. Yeah." He stares straight ahead. No shock. No recoiling, not much of a reaction at all for that matter, as if there were dozens of murdered strippers in his past. Oh, that one? Short hair, petite? Oh yes, of course, Ashley!

"That was a loooong time ago." He takes a sip of his drink.

Okay. And . . . I let the silence—the club music, the girls squealing next to us—stretch out. Still nothing. "I'm not sure I'll be able to tell you much," he says, glancing at the opening band clearing the stage after their set ends. "I don't even remember when that was . . . Were we still living uptown?" He trails off. Not evasively. Not "Let's change the subject." Just flat. Detached. Whatever. His fingers squeeze tighter around my waist.

Wait, what? It had never occurred to me that he might not have anything to say. It was all so crazy! Of course he'd have thought about her over the years. That exceedingly weird night, the 3D porn movie, Ashton Kutcher, the resulting fallout with his girlfriend, the strange feeling of crossing paths, of being intimate, with someone who's now dead. Really? Nothing? How often does this kind of thing happen to people?

"Yeah. Uptown," I say slowly.

I feel silly, confused. A slow, tingly realization starts taking shape that the weight, the regret, the hindsight I had attached to all this was mine alone. To Oliver the situation was just one of many blips that had happened ten years ago in another time, another place. Imagine all the people who had come and gone through his life since then. How could he be expected to remember one random one-night stand from when he was twenty-five?

How naive of me. Of course he couldn't. Oliver hadn't been caught off guard by my big revelation because it simply wasn't one. He didn't look surprised or sheepish. He didn't shift in his seat or abruptly cease hitting on me. I was the one for whom the switch had been flipped. It was I who was now staring at him, vulnerable, searching, while he sat back calmly drinking a beer, just looking ahead to a good time with a girl who'd come to town, like all those years ago, like when Ashley had parachuted into his living room.

The rest of the night is a blur of drinks and dizziness and fleeting moments of connection. The headlining band goes on, we move to the center of the floor. A bit of dancing, a bit of feeling Oliver's hips behind me as I stand facing the stage. The music is anthemic, passionate—at least it sounds that way to me. There are heavy bass notes and insistent keyboards, and when I close my eyes I feel the rhythm in my chest and my ass and between my legs. The beat of the kick drum connects with my heart. I feel overwhelmed. The set ends, and Oliver takes my hand. Where are we going? We leave the club and walk a few blocks to a place you enter from an alleyway where the people are very drunk. Perhaps I am, too?

There's Latin music playing and Oliver appears with mojitos and suddenly a woman is gesturing to me. I should dance with her, it is decided. I should take her hand and let her spin me haphazardly around the small space of floor in front of us while her boyfriend smirks approvingly. Oliver is wearing a similar expression to the guy, slouching against his seat back with one leg up on a nearby chair. I feel self-conscious, but I play it off like I'm the amused straight man while this woman undulates her hips. Do I touch her? Do I smile when she grabs my arm and pulls a bit too hard as she loses her balance? There is no protocol in place here. I am relieved when the song ends and I can excuse myself to reconnect with my mojito. More and more I am feeling like Oliver and I might go home together, and somehow a tiny beam of light within me understands that this is less and less of a good idea.

When had all of this happened? Not just with Oliver but with sex in general. I had trouble with its insistence on setting the agenda. It all felt relatively new to me, this potential to create and destroy at will. The men, everywhere, they seemed to be always looking at you, always available, always so receptive to the slightest bit of attention and always game for bad decisions. You could just pick one, any one at any time in any bar or subway car, and it could turn out to be a spectacular, painful disaster, but no one seemed to know which it would be and no one for sure ever attempted to stop you.

You could take your old pal, a guy who'd known you as a very young woman and respected you and kept his distance, a guy who'd slept with your now-dead childhood best friend and left her disappointed because he'd behaved like all the rest, a guy you haven't seen in nearly a decade. You could take that complicated, messy history and turn it on its head just by, say, drunkenly sitting in his lap in some crappy basement club. He would just have to squeeze your hip and his other hand might brush the hair off your shoulder and then the air would suddenly get heavy.

"You really do have beautiful eyes," he might say, staring into them. And you've heard that one too many times before in too many crappy basement clubs and are hungry for an alternative, but you know that it means a spell has been cast and that all you have to do is smile. Sip your drink and glance at your shoes and turn off the voices in your head that are telling you this is cheap this is cliché this is how the dominoes start falling.

The stakes are even lower with strangers, the voices in your head almost nonexistent. You could probably change the narrative entirely with that guy across the room, the one with the off-balance date and expectant smile. That one would be easy; you're from out of town. Perhaps it might cause a fight with them later or even a breakup, but at the moment none of that would matter, none of that would add up to anything at all.

Maybe at first it felt like a fun magic trick, a power play, a portal to another world, but eventually it becomes an annoyance, a burden even. The telegraphing of availability and receptiveness was a constant thing to manage, a feeling that giving just a little—a friendly nod, a "How was your weekend?" to the guy in the elevator, a hand brushing a knee for an extra second at the bar—could set you down a path where there'd be consequences to deal with. Not huge ones, necessarily, but ones that would interrupt your day or your night, or add up to lasting anger and hurt. Consequences that would make you avoid certain streets and people. Consequences that would make you second-guess your clothes, your shoes, your choices. Consequences that over time would close you up a bit, have you holding your breath, staring straight ahead, pinching your smile at the root and anticipating the worst.

It was something that had taken me most of my twenties to come to terms with, as I gained confidence in myself and with men from the office to the dating world, but Ashley had understood it at twenty-one, I realized now—probably earlier—and for the most part she'd seemed to handle it with equal parts excitement and world-weariness. It wasn't as fun as it looked, that knowledge, the recognition that just about anyone could be reduced to a common denominator if given the chance. She was young to lose that wonder, that sense that, hey, maybe, just maybe, he'll turn out to be great. Sometimes you wished that people would surprise you a little more.

• • •

Did I want Oliver to surprise me? Part of me wanted to push ahead, to be with him for the simple reason that Ashley had done it, too. Maybe that would mean something. That sleeping with him would connect me to her. That when he touched me I'd get to feel what she'd felt, hear the sounds he made that she had heard, see what she must have seen with his body on top of mine. I'd get to be thirty and twenty at once, and maybe all the time in between, too. I'd be experienced and vulnerable and present in the moment with some of me still reaching back through the years to my former self and her former self, falling asleep beside him just as she had done a decade ago. But then what?

A tightness begins to spread between my eyes. I've lost touch with what my body wants and what I thought I came here to do. I feel alone, and I don't want to make my own choices anymore. The thought of walking back to the Ace in my too-high heels feels overwhelming. I am a long way from home, and I am tired.

The next morning I wake up alone. My head pounds. I consider disappearing and cutting my trip short, heading to the airport without a good-bye, but Oliver has already planned to leave work early and take me on a hike in the late afternoon, and I don't want to deal with changing plans. I want to pretend that last night happened exactly as I had intended it to—maybe in the process I'd even convince myself it was true. I put on yesterday's dress and flat sandals and walk up Western Avenue, past the coffee shops and condos and tourists lined up at Pike Place Market.

When I reach City Hall Park, I choose a spot of grass to try for a hungover nap in the sun. Nearby, what I gradually gather to be a homeless outreach group is moving gingerly among the single people posted up under trees, many of them with tarps and garbage bags, holding their possessions. "Would you like a brown bag lunch?" the volunteers are asking earnestly. "We have fresh fruit, sandwiches, and water." My eyes are closed and the voices are growing closer, and suddenly they are above me.

"Would you like some food?" asks a gentle-looking girl in her twenties. "We have fresh fruit, sandwiches, and water."

"No, thank you," I say. Do they actually think I'm homeless, or are they just trying to be inclusive? It doesn't matter. I feel shame and validation all at once.

Oliver is driving us to Franklin Falls, a hiking spot about an hour outside the city along the Snoqualmie River. It's cloudy, and I'm sipping from a water bottle, still dehydrated and a bit fuzzy from my hangover. My jeans feel tight.

The air in Oliver's car is thick. The radio is on, and I'm staring out the window at the greenery rushing by and telling myself that it's all okay. I think of Ashley and how she's led me here. What an absurd, confounding thought. My friend, eight years dead, is dictating my thoughts, my movements, my trips across the country, and, yes, my attractions from the grave. What would she make of all of this? What would she make of me?

This is all part of the process, my mind is saying, grasping for trite aphorisms like a newbie yoga teacher. The process of what exactly, I'm not sure, but I try to console myself with the fact that this will soon be over. Spending a final afternoon with Oliver, this too shall pass. People disappoint you in the most unexpected of ways; it doesn't have to be your fault. Hurt people hurt people. Mojitos are gross.

It's as if we have nothing to say, but actually there is plenty, we're just choosing to say none of it. Some thoughts I'm not verbalizing include: maybe this—me finding Oliver, me being in this car—wasn't such a good idea. Maybe Oliver and I shouldn't keep in touch after this. Maybe I don't actually like this guy after all, and maybe I never did. Why does this feel like that weekend with Ashley all over again?

•   •   •

The night had ended on a confusing, bitter note, with long-ago dynamics sealed in amber somehow emerging again into view. It was nearing last call, and we had passed the moment where something could have reasonably happened in good faith with enthusiasm and spontaneity. We were into sour-stomached, hedging-our-bets territory, but neither of us was quite ready to let go. A bit of jockeying for position was occurring. By that point I had decided I'd prefer for Oliver to simply make a move and for me to decline than for us to actually go through with anything. Was I attracted to him in earnest, or did I just want to win?

For his part, Oliver appeared to be rapidly losing his patience. He suddenly remembered aloud a woman he had recently started sleeping with, Lauren. This was the first mention of her. She was younger, and had been a friend for a long time—had even been at his wedding. Nick had hit on her. Oliver and she had gotten quite close, actually, even before Oliver had left his wife, but the marriage had essentially been over by then anyway. He felt a little bit guilty, but not really. His wife had been hurt by the divorce, he hadn't been. It had all been his decision, and it was the right one.

Was I missing something? Earlier in the night Oliver had said he was only a few weeks out of his marital home, that he felt shell-shocked, unstable. That he didn't even have a new bed yet—he'd been sleeping on a futon. Earlier in the night, he had seemed like a reasonable guy, one I understood. Why was he telling me this now?

It was nearing 2 a.m., and I could still feel all the places his hands had touched me in the preceding hours. Our thighs were pressed together, and I instinctively backed away.

"Stop looking at me like that," he said.

"Like what?"

"You know."

Oh, did I? I thought I was looking at him the exact same way he had been looking at me, if not a bit more skeptically. That the mirror neurons in the back of my brain were just reflecting back the buzzy, flirtatious, will-we-or-won't-we energy he had been giving off all night, rolling it around in a loop and shooting it back out again with occasional detours into second-guessing. This was not something I could do on my own.

If I were a slapper—I wish I were a slapper—this would have been the moment. But instead I was stunned and had misplaced my voice. Oliver didn't let up: it's not cool, he said. If Lauren or one of her friends saw us right now, he'd be really embarrassed. And all of this was my fault, clearly. What the fuck.

How quickly the once-mighty buzz had fallen. A tiny part of me recognized that Oliver was condescending to me, throwing off a sense of shame and feeling of rejection within him and pasting it onto me because he couldn't deal with it. That I had done nothing wrong, neither had he, really—well, until then—but that truly if one of us had behaved badly, it was he.

Alas, it was a small part only. In the moment, the trick worked. His decidedly cocky, reactive move, what I later understand to be a textbook dose of gaslighting, knocked the wind right out of me. I felt stung, unprotected, not chosen yet again.

At the beginning of the night I'd thought I was a woman, but suddenly I was a girl again. I was self-conscious and ashamed and swallowing the labels some dipshit was applying to me because he was older and a man, and he had a bigger ego that assisted him in talking down to people. I remembered the way Ashley had stone-faced the guys when we had been out for drinks in Manhattan and later, Nick. She'd kept her power; she'd raised the game.

She would not have stood for this, I felt sure of it.

I got up, an attempt to regain some sense of stability, but I was wobbly in my shoes. I grabbed the railing on the nearby wall and looked toward the door. There were smokers gathered on the sidewalk, laughter, couples pressed into each other as they walked.

On the trail the ground is slippery and my Converse sneakers do not offer much traction. Oliver and I are climbing in silence up a sloping, wooded path with trees all around us and branches overhead and moss-covered rocks to hop between. A few people are descending as we're on our way up; most nod in that friendly, earnest hiker way as they pass us. How do we look to them? A sullen couple: the woman with her hands in her pockets, staring straight down at the dirt beneath her feet. The man, pinched and dutiful, occasionally looking back to see that she's okay, but mostly he's in his own head. What's their deal? What could make them so uptight in the middle of the woods?

More steps get climbed, and there's a steep little hill to scale, and then just like that the trees open up and we are there. The waterfall is stunning. It's loud and rushing and calming all at once, white rapids pouring over dark rocks from high overhead, the wet surface slicked with murky algae. For a moment my mind is mesmerized. A bubble of mist surrounds us, with light breaking through the clouds catching the droplets here and there, making the air appear to sparkle. I have given up on protecting my hair, my once-sleek blowout now a mess of damp and matted frizz. There's no going back. We walk to a clearing where there's a couple with kids, and I'm looking at the sky and Oliver is beside me and suddenly everyone else is gone.

"Ashley pushed me down on my bed when we got home that night," he says out of nowhere. "She tore my clothes off." A long pause. "To be honest, I was sketched out." The words hang in the air. I want to shove them back where they came from. This feels wrong, even though techni-cally it's what I want to hear—the intimacies, the insider knowledge I could never have been there for. But we are in nature, and I don't want this anymore, not now, not this way. Not so callously, not after last night. This isn't fair.

"At the time it was the best blow job I had ever gotten," he says. Oh god. No. No. No. Please. "And then in the morning, her hair was all over the place, and that was endearing." I want him to stop. I hope he stops. There couldn't be more.

We're both looking out at the falls, and I don't know how to react. What would an appropriate follow-up question be to this? There isn't one. And suddenly I know this is over. I can't make myself ask any more, feel any more, go through any more with this man. He has nothing else for me, and I have nothing else for him. I had hoped to get a glimpse of a private Ashley I had never seen, but instead what I got was another void—a somewhat disrespectful one at that. Oliver wasn't the person here who knew Ashley intimately; that was me. The depth of the memories I had of her were mine alone—to him she was just a barely recollected one-night stand.

Oliver wouldn't be leading me anywhere; I would have to lead myself.

I look at him now, all of him. Our eyes connect, and I notice how blue his are. I notice his receding hairline and the sideburns I used to love. I think of how we first met ten years ago on a warm summer night this month, when we were young and New York was brand-new. Before 9/11, before Nick would be the first to break my heart, before Ashley would take her last breath. I am sad.

Oliver turns and begins walking off the deck and I follow him, cursing as I lose my footing a bit on the first few steps up the next hill. "Walk in front of me," he calls out, saying he'll catch me if I slip again. "I'll be right behind you."

8

GOOD LUCK TO YOU

THE NEXT STOP was Los Angeles. It had to be. It was crazy it had taken me this long to get here. It's September 30, 2009. The GPS in my compact from Hertz leads me down the 405 while the radio blares aggressive rap. I've never rented a car before or driven in this city, so just making it to the Airport Courthouse on time feels like a minor triumph. The city is charged with a sunny energy that the East Coast couldn't dream of having—it's magic hour all day long.

After Oliver and Seattle, I had taken a few months to process everything. Seeing him had left me bitter and annoyed, as much at myself as at him. It wasn't supposed to go like that! I was supposed to be on a truth-seeking journey and in control, what was going on? I thought about giving up entirely.

But then I remembered how I'd felt on that cold fall day in 2008 when my LexisNexis search had turned up reports that a suspect had been charged with Ashley's murder. I had been scared and excited and felt as though I were on the cusp of some path forward toward the next stage of my life. My childhood was dead, and there was an alleged serial killer attached to the whole mess. I couldn't just leave it at that; I had to find a new story, a bigger story, both for me and for her. Fuck Oliver. He wouldn't be the end. He wasn't even the beginning.

Another ex–crime reporter friend at work helped me with the next steps. Although I had worked in media for some time—I currently edited our magazine's online travel, restaurant, and events sections—nothing in my background had prepared me for this. I should call the court system's Media Relations Division, my friend said, and ask about the next date on the docket. She had even told me what to say: "Hi, I'd like to find out the next court date for case number SA068002, Michael Gargiulo." That was it. A different friend of a friend inside the Los Angeles County District Attorney's Office had given me the defendant's name and case number, so I had that much to go on. I didn't know if real reporters or investigators or whoever else actually called the Media Relations Division actually spoke that way, if using the case number that way would out me as a rube, but I went with it. I said it just like that, holding my breath all the while. "Oh, the serial guy?" asked the operator on the other end of the line, gum chewing implied but not audible. "Hang on a minute." I hung on, and when she returned I wrote down what she said on the back of my reporter's notebook at my desk at work. There would be a pretrial hearing in a few months' time, at the Airport Courthouse on La Cienega. That was all there was to say. I didn't know exactly what that meant, but I knew I would be there.

My DA friend explained a little bit more. California is a death penalty state, and the prosecution was asking for Gargiulo to receive the death penalty. Death penalty trials are different from typical murder trials in a few key ways; cases take longer to actually get to trial—often more than a year—and the trial itself has two parts instead of one: the guilt phase and the penalty phase. Prosecutors and defense attorneys prepare for both parts of the trial at once, and there are often twice as many attorneys for both sides during proceedings. Before the case could go to trial, the state would have to prove probable cause, which would happen in something called a preliminary hearing, which is sort of a minitrial without a jury. And before all that, there would be numerous, shorter pre-preliminary court appearances for both sides to discuss the discovery process and other issues. I was about to attend one of those.

I had been to LA only once before, in my early twenties, to the funeral of my then boyfriend's grandmother. We'd flown in late and stayed in some shitty motel near the airport and cabbed it straight to the service in Santa Monica and back. I can still picture the lit-up colors of the Ferris wheel on the water as we passed, the families and couples licking ice cream on the boardwalk, my black funeral dress creased and sweaty. This time I'm here on my own, with a rented car and a spot on my friend's couch and a suitcase full of versatile warm-weather outfits.

The building looks nothing like what I was expecting. Instead of marble, columns, and Latin inscriptions like I'm used to from New York, this place is early-nineties office-park style with ten floors of blue reflective glass and a clear elevator you can see going up and down from outside. There are palm trees and parking meters that tell me I'll need approximately twenty-eight quarters to make it through the day.

Inside Department 100 on the eighth floor, the scene feels workaday and a little hectic. Harried DAs, detectives, and witnesses shuffle in and out, everyone lost in his or her own agenda. There are more than a dozen cases on the docket that day, and there doesn't seem to be an order to what's going when. The judge is a sassy sort, given to proclamations that vacillate between bored annoyance and parental sincerity. "This is your chance to go out and make a better life," she tells one female defendant, released after being an accomplice to a drug crime. To another, sentenced to ten years for a repeat offense of robbery and violent assault, she gives barely a glance.

I sit in the back row and try to be inconspicuous. Courts make me anxious as a rule—regardless of why I'm there. I always feel just a step away from being fined, ticketed, or arrested for some infraction I wasn't aware I was committing. Hours go by, and I wonder if I might have missed everything when I went down to feed the meter. A bizarre hearing is going on, which I glean has something to do with identity theft. "The defendant was going through a divorce," says her lawyer, "and met a woman at Ruby's who told her she knew an easy way to make some extra money." I zone out. An overweight man in a wheelchair is pushed in by his younger, ponytailed aide. Both of them converse with the clerk, and the older man appears flustered. There's a pause, and they exchange glances with the judge.

"All right, let's just bring Gargiulo in," the judge says tiredly. Everything suddenly snaps into focus. My heart starts beating fast enough to make me feel off balance, and then the bailiff opens a side door and in walks a skinny, hunched guy wearing an orange state prison jumpsuit. He looks dried out, vulnerable, nothing like the menacing face I had held in my mind or the snide image from his mug shot. He is utterly unremarkable, just another white male anybody I might have passed on the street and forgotten a moment later.

Is this the man who stabbed Ashley forty-seven times? Is this the person who crushed her skull and left her to bleed to death on that cream-colored carpet? I try to picture what he might have looked like gripping the knife, standing over her, but I can see his hands only the way they are now: cuffed and impotent.

The wheelchair-bound man turns out to be Gargiulo's defense

attorney, Charles Lindner, and the ponytailed man, his paralegal and son. Later, I would google him and learn that, according to his website, he had been part of O. J. Simpson's Dream Team and had cowritten the defense closing arguments for the case. Legal jargon is batted back and forth between the judge and the DA. I strain to hear and comprehend, but all I can pick up is dates and numbers. I look around to see if anyone else is paying attention, but they're not. In just under two minutes, the scene I traveled three thousand miles to witness is over.

The judge issues a continuance, and Gargiulo's next appearance is set for a few weeks later. Her parting words for him are brief but echoing, and she hasn't said them to anyone else all day. I realize in that moment that they're the same ones I've been wanting to hear myself: "Good luck to you."

PART

THREE

9

EVERYTHING IN
RETROSPECT

LOTS OF FUZZY math gets thrown around when you talk about the dead. Words are spoken slowly. Sentences come out in the second and third person conditional; phrases whip up politeness and magical thinking into an airy soufflé that falls flat if you look at it the wrong way.

"It would have meant a lot to her to know you were here," Detective Thomas Small told me on the first day of Gargiulo's preliminary hearing in June 2010. This was the first time I was meeting the detective, but I recognized his name immediately from Ashley's coroner's report. I didn't tell him that.

It had been about nine months since the first court appearance I attended, dizzy and biting my cuticles, not making eye contact with anyone.

Now I was back. Looking up. Speaking, albeit slowly. Trying to meet curious gazes squarely in hopes that a sense of confidence would follow. I was introducing myself as Ashley's friend, but what did that really mean at this point? I was still coming to terms with the answer and how I fit into the criminal proceeding that was soon to unfold.

I was about to meet a whole cast of Hollywood characters and learn details about the last year of Ashley's life that before I could only have imagined, but I didn't know any of that yet. I didn't yet know that in a few days I'd find myself outside this very building, squinting up at the afternoon sun and looking desperately for a sign about what to do next. I didn't yet know that I'd hear things about Ashley so surprising, so unbelievable, that I'd wonder whether I might have been hallucinating.

All I knew at that moment was that I had made it this far and I would continue putting one foot in front of the other until I came up with a better idea.

"It would have meant a lot to her to know you were here." I considered that. It had been ten years since I'd last seen Ashley (nine of which she'd been dead for), and I was now at the preliminary hearing for the man who'd likely killed her, who was also accused of killing another woman and attempting to kill a third.

It was a clear, sunny Los Angeles day outside, but what did it matter? Ashley was dead, and therefore she couldn't think or feel anything. And the reason I was here was because she was dead. If she wasn't dead, I doubt I would have been in this city at all—I certainly wouldn't have been in this courthouse. Maybe Ashley and I would be having margaritas right now down the street—downtown LA is a happening neighborhood now, can you believe it?—or maybe we'd be getting pedicures or smoothies or whatever else you do with your old friend of twenty years. I wouldn't know—Ashley was the last one I had.

I knew it was just a thing you say and that the detective had meant something kind, but I interpreted it as more like a logic puzzle. The sentence made me feel caught in my throat and full of adrenaline, even though it inherently made no sense. What was the best way to hold two mutually exclusive ideas in my head at the same time? Ashley was dead . . . but it still meant a lot to her; I was in a courthouse . . . because she wasn't. After you die, it seemed to assume, what you want is for people to care—to ask questions about your passing, to rant and rave against the unfairness of it all. Not to let go easily. That's what would make you happy. Right?

If I had been murdered, would it make me happy to know that my childhood best friend had taken vacation days from her job—because we were adults now, we had jobs—to fly across the country and rent a car and put on a tasteful dress and closed-toe heels and show up in a courthouse almost a decade after I'd died to find out what had happened? Or would I just be like, "Aw, that's cool of you, for sure, but maybe just stick with what you're doing; make chicken for dinner, fuck your boyfriend, plan a summer trip. Have an extra glass of wine for me, and watch the sun set. This all sucks and you can't change that, so you may as well carry on, my friend. Remember the good times we had, forget about the crappy ones. They were all so long ago, anyway. And hey, actually, it's great up here— you'll love it! Michael Jackson just arrived not too long ago. Oh, and the food is amazing."

Maybe part of me worried that Ashley would be angry, pissed off, raging. That death and time had hardened her and she had decided the people she left behind deserved the pain they felt because it wasn't nearly as bad as what she'd gotten. Maybe she'd think I was a fraud. "Oh, hi there: go fuck yourself. Am I supposed to believe you've been crying about me all these years? Do you light a candle on my birthday? Do you speak to me at night? Whatever. Where were you when you could have done something? You think this is all exciting now, worthy of your time, but where were you when I was getting stabbed forty-seven times? Or all the times you didn't come out to visit me in California? Millennium New Year's? We went to Melissa Joan Hart's house, and she was wearing some crazy Marie Antoinette getup! Where were you when I turned twenty-two? Like what you're doing here matters at all. Seriously. Have a great time listening to all this bullshit—it won't change anything."

It was hard to imagine Ashley coming from a place of bitterness, though—she had never been like that in life. Bitchy sometimes, yes. Cynical, sure. But not bitter. Though who knows what being murdered does to a person? Maybe it could flip you into another dimension altogether, make you totally unrecognizable by the people who once knew you. Maybe your clothes wouldn't even fit the same way. Maybe your eyes changed color, maybe you could see into people's souls. Maybe you were the one who decided who would live and die now, and how you made the call would change based on what you ate for lunch. The weather's always perfect in this infinite hypothetical thought loop, though; you could stay here for weeks.

But before all of that, I was twenty minutes early. Everything had changed since the last continuance I had attended—the judge, the prosecutor, all of it—we were in the big leagues now. The new courthouse downtown was huge and dark, with paparazzi at the ready slinking along the perimeter. We were in the same building where the O. J. Simpson murder trial had taken place. I had been sixteen during that trial, a senior at Exeter, with a sexy older girl from Bogotá named Silvia as a roommate. I was so sure he'd be found guilty that I had bet my friends that if O.J. was acquitted, I'd ask out the boy I had a crush on, Tom, a curly-haired hippie who played the banjo and had done a semester away on a farm in Vermont. He'd said yes, then later stood me up.

Phil Spector was tried for the murder of Lana Clarkson on this same floor. It was the maximum-security floor; I had to go through another round of metal detectors after getting off the elevator even though I had already cleared the ones downstairs. Lindsay Lohan would show up at this building multiple times, and across the street was where the Charles Manson murders were tried in 1970. If you were famous and did something wrong in LA, you'd find your way here eventually, it seemed.

After seeing Gargiulo in court I had spent a few months letting it all sink in. How far would I take this? I still didn't know. It felt as though the stakes would only be mounting as time went on. What would be next: interviewing Gargiulo? Seeing the trial – whenever that would be— through to the end? I couldn't imagine handling all of that, but I put those thoughts aside and focused on as many baby steps as I could think of. I focused on the big questions that had kept me in the room: How did Ashley and I start out so similar and end up in such different places? The motto of my fancy boarding school that I had nearly flunked out of—*Finis origine pendet*, the end depends on the beginning—was that really all there was to it? If that were really true, why was she dead while I was still here?

Back in New Jersey earlier in the year, I had reconnected with some of Ashley's and my grade school friends, and a few of them who were still local had even met me for drinks. A guy who had become a video game designer said the clearest thing he could remember about either of us was that we were always together.

"Ashley was cool without trying," said Sarah as we sat in her family's dining room while her son played in the next room. There were references to outfits I had forgotten—that jean jacket she always wore!—or a flash of her personality that would make the loss feel fresh all over again. There were a few tears and a few laughs, though nothing happened that really broke anything wide open. Mostly I came away feeling lucky that the years had gone for us in the way that they had. As adrift as we might have felt from time to time, we were alive.

I visited our childhood piano teacher, the woman who had taught us duets side by side for years. She was semiretired now, but it turned out she had saved a copy of every program from every student recital she had ever hosted, stretching way back into the eighties. She pulled a few of them from when Ashley and I had played together and we looked at them silently on her couch. "Did Ashley keep up with the piano, do you know?" she asked, her cat leaping across my lap.

I kept calling the Media Relations Division every few months and mostly just heard about more continuances, and then all of a sudden something bigger was on the horizon: the preliminary hearing, that minitrial without a jury. I wrote the information down in the same notebook I had been keeping things in at my desk and then put it aside. It was the end of winter, my birthday would be a in a few weeks, and soon the icebergs of gray sludge that had become a permanent fixture on the New York sidewalks would slowly start to shrink until one day pretty much overnight it would be back to bike rides and bare legs and the long winter would feel like one of those bad dreams you still sometimes thought about even though the sense memory had long since loosened its grip.

"June 21. Clara Shortridge Foltz Criminal Justice Center, 210 West Temple St, Dept. 108." The words represented a time and place thousands of miles and dozens of days away. It felt almost as abstract as the idea of my father's or mother's death—a sad thing, a true thing, a thing that was an eventual inevitability but that I'd rather not consider too deeply in the present. The time would come when it would come, and I would deal with it then.

I looked at the notebook on and off for a few weeks, sometimes in the morning, sometimes before I left for the night. I wrote down notes from meetings, telephone messages, and random ink scrawlings of arrows and stars on the same page. I copied the information into an Excel document on my office computer where I had begun compiling relevant names and contacts. There were lawyers and coroners and press secretaries on that list. There were private investigators and sheriff's detectives, too. I bought a new case for my laptop. It was bright and had handles like a briefcase, and when I carried it I felt as though I were going places. I googled Clara Shortridge Foltz. She had been a famous suffragette and the first female lawyer in California. After her husband had left her and her five children, she'd gone on to become to become the first woman admitted to the California bar and had later run for governor at the age of eighty-one.

"Everything in retrospect seems weird, phantasmal, and unreal. I peer back across the misty years into that era of prejudice and limitation, when a woman lawyer was a joke . . . but the story of my triumphs will eventually disclose that though the battle has been long and hard-fought it was worthwhile," she wrote.

I decided that Clara Shortridge Foltz would be my spirit animal, and after a few more days I booked a flight and found a friend with an extra room to stay with in Hollywood and rented a car and pulled my hair back and practiced the "square breathing" technique I'd once read about—inhale, hold, exhale, hold, over and over and over—while I walked through the door and into the elevator and through the second security check right up to where I was. Inhale, hold, exhale, hold, over and over and over.

As I walked down the hall that first morning, I had no idea that in just a few minutes I would meet three very important people all at once: Detective Small; Jennifer DiSisto, Ashley's roommate at the time of her death; and Christopher Duran, a stylist who introduced himself as Ashley's best friend. All I saw was a group sitting on benches lining the walls up ahead, but I wasn't close enough yet to see their faces. My thoughts pinballed around my brain: Were those her parents? What did they look like these days? What should I say to them? What would they say to me?

Suddenly I was back in Ashley's parents' kitchen in New Jersey, pressing out tiny, misshapen cookies as Ashley mixed up icing next to me. I think of Ashley's mother's hair: dark, thick, straight, and shiny. Cynthia Ellerin looked like her daughter, and her daughter looked like her—not like my mother and me. They were a pair, the two of them: brown hair, brown eyes, delicate features, and slender limbs.

I had written to the Ellerins again a few weeks prior to leaving for this trip. I thought of Ashley all the time, I told them, and I was going to California to attend the preliminary hearing. Would they be there? Could we meet? I'd had no idea how they'd respond, given that they hadn't replied to any of the notes I had sent in the years following Ashley's death. I'd never taken it personally. I didn't fool myself that I had some magic words to say or that hearing from me would make anything better. It had to hurt, that much I understood, but still I wanted them to know that I was remembering her. That felt like something to me that was worth putting out there; whether they acknowledged it or not didn't matter.

This time I included my email address and cell phone number, though, two things that hadn't existed the last time I'd seen them. Maybe that would make it easier? Another old friend of Ashley's I'd connected with earlier in the year told me that she also hadn't been in touch with the Ellerins since the murder and that she had heard from others that contact with people from Ashley's past was too painful for them.

Still, I continued to write once in a while, and so did my mother, who sent holiday cards to the family regularly. It had been nine years now, and I wondered if maybe something would be different this time. At least if I saw them in the courthouse, I didn't want it to come as a surprise. But by the time I'd left New York, I hadn't heard anything.

So many times had I pictured seeing the Ellerins again, at their house in California or back in New Jersey for some unknown reason or—since Ashley's been gone—in a huge, sterile government building in Los Angeles. I wondered whether I'd burst into tears or whether they would.

I wondered if I'd recognize her mother's smell when she hugged me. Or maybe she wouldn't hug me at all. She'd avoid eye contact or glare at me with pain. Maybe they were angry at me for being there, angry that this was happening at all and that people were allowed to come see it. This wasn't my place. This was a family matter. And why was I here now instead of being there then? Why had she lost her daughter and my mother hadn't?

In my more narcissistic fantasies, I wondered if perhaps her parents might look at me as a shadow daughter. *I am almost the exact same age as your daughter would have been had she lived.* Maybe for her parents looking at me would feel like having a phantom limb—a phantom grown child. For a second, they would almost see their daughter at the age she would have been had she grown up to be the age I am now. I would be the promise she didn't get to realize. I had made it out of childhood, the teenage years, and even young adulthood. I had been lucky so far, and she had not.

I'd had a dream a few months earlier that her father had appeared at a neighborhood party back in New Jersey. He'd smiled at me and looked young. We'd caught up about things—my family, his—and it had been okay. He'd treated me as an adult. The truth had been in the background, but we had been facing each other in the present. *That wasn't so bad*, I'd thought, and then I'd woken up. In my bedroom in the gray violet early morning light I'd felt comforted and hopeful for a moment. How nice it can be when dreams play pretend.

I walked farther down the hall, and the faces came into focus. They were strangers, only. I felt able to breathe in a new way. I could stay anonymous. I could take out my laptop and pretend to be a paralegal or a reporter. I could fake it, I could keep this going. I could handle this. I sat down on a bench next to three people about my age, a woman and two men.

Of course I was listening to them and pretending not to. They chatted with familiarity; two of them seemed to be a couple. There was a woman about my age, pretty with brown hair; her boyfriend was a bit more casual with a ponytail. The third, the guy closest to me, was neatly dressed with closely cropped salt-and-pepper hair, skinny pants, and a nervous energy. I caught pieces of words, short bursts of distracted laughter. They were catching up. They hadn't seen each other in quite some time. I thought I heard the name Ashley—or is it Ashton?—but assumed it was a coincidence. A few moments later, the same thing happened.

It was not a coincidence.

One of them had heard from Ashton not too long before. "It's crazy that the press called her his girlfriend," one was saying. "Ashley used to laugh about that," the skinny-pants guy said. "I'm not that guy's girlfriend," he said, speaking through Ashley, imitating her tone: deep sarcasm, bored amusement. I was confused, but they were here for her, too, that was certain.

The realization was thrilling and terrifying all at once. It felt as if I had heard someone speaking English for the first time after months of wandering by myself in the Himalayas. Part of me wanted to call out, to say "Hello, hi—I exist, too! We're part of the same tribe!" But another part had the inclination to hold back: I'd gotten this far on my own, perhaps it was better to keep it that way. Perhaps I should just keep taking everything in and gathering it up and saving it for later to parse it out in private.

But then a moment later I felt frustrated with myself—I should be pushing through all this discomfort, all this fear. That's what Ashley would want. Wouldn't she? She might not have understood what I was doing here, but of course she would see us all across the room and say, "Oh wow, that's my friend and those are my friends, and do you all know each other? You should meet." And then there'd be hugs and introductions and commonalities exchanged and California-style small talk, and new bonds, however fleeting, would be formed. That part seemed clear, even if nothing else did. The story, the scenes, the situations I had sat with in my head alone for years were suddenly bursting out into the land of the living. This was one of those moments that would separate things into a before and after.

"Are y'all going to room 108?" I mumbled tentatively.

What the fuck. Why did I say y'all? I was from New Jersey. And it had taken me a long time to come up with that one.

They answered right away. They were kind and seemed weary. The woman said they were there to testify, and she asked what my story was. I said I was a childhood friend of Ashley's from New York. I spoke to the woman in particular but moved to make eye contact with them all.

"Did they fly you out here?" she asked.

"I came on my own," I said, confused, and then I realized that they thought I was here to testify as well. For a moment I wished I were testifying; then at least I'd have a clear and easily digestible answer to the question of what I was doing there, even if it was just a way to pass.

"Oh wow," she said. "Why?"

Before I could think too much about it, the simple line tumbled out, no southern affectations this time: "I want to know what happened." It felt like one of the truest things I'd said in a while.

A man with a badge appears, and greets the woman warmly. I learn that her name is Jen. She's the one who found Ashley's body, says the skinny-pants guy to me as an aside. His name is Chris. He calls himself Ashley's best friend and says they hung out every single day, and he explains that he introduced Jen to Ashley when she needed a new roommate. He introduces me to the man with the badge, whose name is Detective Small. He is kind to me, chatting about where I'm from and my job back home.

I sit on the bench in the hallway outside the courtroom next to the detective, fluorescent lights turning everything sallow. He's a nice-looking man, tall and stocky with a gray mustache and a neatly pressed suit. He wears a chunky braided wedding band, and he looks a bit like the fifth-grade teacher Ashley and I had for social studies, Mr. Reilly. He'd be right at home coaching a kids' Little League game or flipping burgers on the backyard grill, Bud Light in one hand, spatula in the other.

It's hard to reconcile that he's also someone who has the sights and sounds of violence, chaos, and danger burned into his brain. I assume that he's fired a gun, been at crime scenes, broken through doors. He's seen a dead body, lots of them probably. He saw Ashley's, twisted and inanimate, splayed across her living room floor nine years ago. In fact, he's never seen her any other way.

Back on the hallway bench, Chris still seems nervous; he's breathing quickly while crossing and uncrossing his legs and checking his phone and adjusting his pants. I can relate, even though I don't have to go on the stand in a few minutes and speak the truth (my truth?) in front of a judge and lawyers and a handcuffed, jumpsuited accused murderer. Both Chris and Jen are wondering when someone named Justin is going to show up; neither one of them has spoken to him in quite a while.

As I take them in for a few more minutes, I'm realizing it's actually hard to tell if Chris and Jen are actually friends anymore. There's a stiffness to their interactions, and I'm wondering if perhaps the familiarity they're sharing now is really just a relic.

Later, Chris would tell me that he and Jen had been very close for a time before Ashley's death but that the murder had broken everything—and everyone—up. Emotions had run high, and rumors had flown around about who had said what to whom, and it had gotten to be easier for everyone to just keep their distance.

I would learn that this actually was the first time they were seeing each other in many years, and eventually they'd find their way back to what had brought them together in the first place. In between talking to detectives and press and appearing in hearings and eventually the trial, they'd travel to Italy together, drink at the Standard, and remember Ashley long into the night.

The guy next to Jen is her boyfriend, and he is there for moral support. He's laid back, not dressed for court. Jen clutches his hand tightly as Detective Small chats with her about what will happen in the courtroom. He has a binder with him, and he asks if she'd like to look over her statement again, flipping through it to find the right page. I'm guessing that the binder is the murder book, a thing my crime reporter friend at the office told me about. From my understanding, it's like a big case file investigators use to keep everything together related to a murder: photos, diagrams, witness interviews, forensic reports. It's just the facts, ma'am, but all the facts from all the ma'ams. It's everything they know in one place. I wish so much that I could look through it! I imagine it to be a plethora of information: names, dates, people and places and dark secrets of Ashley's life that I'm only just beginning to scratch at the edges of.

I listen intently to the detective, as though the stuff he's saying applies to me even though I know it does not. I'm not quite one of them. Am I jealous? Just a minute ago, part of me wished I were there to testify so I'd have a more justifiable reason to be appearing in court, and now I am realizing that testifying would carry other significance as well: It would mean I was necessary. It would mean that I would go on record connected to Ashley, that something I knew or the things I could say and the way I'd say them could help her somehow. Find justice? Be remembered? Bring closure? I imagined the words I'd use, whom I'd make eye contact with. Whether my voice would crack. Chris and Jen had suffered a loss, a trauma, but by testifying the two of them had a chance to make something of all of that and carry it forward. I want that, too.

Chris tells me he was there when she met "him"—Michael. I nod in acknowledgment, but inside my brain is exploding and I'm struggling to keep up. Michael told them he repaired furnaces and air-conditioning, and he was in her house a few times. Wait, what? They're referring to "him" as if he were definitely the guy, no question? And they all knew one another? This is terrifying in a brand-new way. The dizzying information is coming hard and fast. The friends, the body, Ashton, all of it. I'm working hard to synthesize this with everything that came before and everything I made assumptions about these past nine years. There's so much more I want to ask, but part of me feels like I need to play it cool, at least for now.

After a few more minutes on the bench, Detective Small goes in to check on something, and when he comes out he tells Chris and Jen they'll probably be up soon, but they need to wait in the hall until they're called. I don't. Witnesses are not allowed to hear others' testimony before they present their own, but me? I can breeze right in and listen to whatever I want. There are no special circumstances or restrictions applied to me. Lucky me.

I look at Jen and Chris and give them a quick shrug. I'm standing to go in when suddenly a floppy-haired, pinstripe-suited burst of California cool breezes down the hall and into our space. For once I don't have to guess at what's going on: Justin has arrived.

Lots of people seem to have some sort of real or self-generated celebrity quality out here; most places you go in LA, it's hard to tell who's famous and who's not. Homeless people are shirtless with six-pack abs. Cool supporting actors from the latest Scorsese movie are eating egg white omelets at grungy diners. If you haven't seen them in a movie you at least feel like you have, and in that way it's like a great equalizer.

Justin is handsome, and that "Is he actually a celebrity?" game starts playing in my head almost unconsciously. Didn't I see him in a Lifetime movie a few weeks ago? Or was it a Wendy's commercial last night? "Hey, guys," he says affably, shuffling from side to side in his Vans slip-ons and doing an uptick nod at the detective. Chris and Jen stay sitting, and it feels as if a beat or two go by before anyone reacts.

Justin has the frenetic energy of a hippie forced to put on a monkey suit for some pitch meeting or family event. The fabric is straining at the seams and his pants are a bit short, exposing his tapered ankles and his brightly colored socks. I'm guessing he surfs. He's almost like comic relief at this point: tall, tan, undeterred, and operating in a completely different emotional ecosystem than the rest of us ordinary folks. I wouldn't have been surprised to hear him say something like, "What's up? Just thought I'd swing through on my way out to Malibu—the waves are supposed to be gnarly right now. Y'all ready to nail this testimony deal? So stoked."

Chris introduces me quickly, and I learn Justin works in the highway billboard business. Who does that? I'm not even sure I know what that means. It sounds absurd. It sounds like a job someone would have in some LA noir story, a pulp paperback. Like private detective or gun moll. Everyone here feels like an invented character, myself included. Chris is a hairstylist, Jen is in the art world, I'm a magazine editor from the East Coast, and preposterously we're all connected by our dead friend— a stripper with a heart of gold—and an alleged serial killer. What would this movie be called? Or would it be a web series or a Showtime original? Would it be a dark buddy comedy or a thriller or an epic journey of self-discovery? The loglines practically wrote themselves.

10

NEVER-ENDING
SWEET SPOT

"WHEN YOU SAY [Ashley] was a party girl, does that go further than going to parties, in terms of your definition?"

Jen takes a breath. She's been on the stand a while now, and the slut-shaming questions about Ashley keep piling up. She remains composed. The defense attorney, Charles Lindner, is the same guy in the wheelchair I saw last year at the continuance at the Airport Courthouse. This time he's got room to move. He's got edge. His phrases drip with sarcasm, literary references, and incredulity. "Do you know, or do you think you know?" is a common one. "Does your memory improve as time goes by?" is another particularly needling barb. He picks at witnesses during cross-examination, parsing words and phrases, catching them in contradictions. They dab at their eyes with tissues, and he continues apace, appearing not to register it. I cringe often and feel thankful to be sitting back here and not up there.

He asks Jen to list the drugs she observed in their apartment—"powder cocaine? crack cocaine?"—and he asks for details on Ashley's sex work, which Jen doesn't seem to have.

"Did Miss Ellerin tell you she was working in Las Vegas?" Jen says yes. She did know that Ashley disappeared on some weekends but did not know the nature of her work beyond "dancing." Lindner insists on referring to it as "pole dancing."

The Vegas part gives me pause. Ashley worked in another state? I remember her talking about her stripping and escorting all those years ago when she visited me in New York, but I always assumed she was doing it closer to home, in LA, though I'm not sure I ever asked for those specifics. Now I have a whole new picture of things, and it saddens me unexpectedly. Something about the thought of Ashley leaving her friends—her home, her life—and flying away to another city for the weekend to work alone, naked, felt unspeakably lonely to me, but perhaps that was part of why she did it that way. Like a cheating husband who never takes his mistress to a restaurant where someone he knows might see them, Ashley didn't want her shadow self to get caught. Perhaps there was an emotional efficiency in keeping parts of herself separate from one another—there'd be no one around to put them all together.

Lindner stays mostly behind the desk, but occasionally he turns his wheelchair in the direction of the jury box even though it's empty. I can only imagine how it will be when an actual jury is in those seats, taking notes, scowling, looking bored. What kind of picture will they be drawing of Ashley in their minds?

When I first entered the courtroom, I didn't anticipate encountering anyone else who was also interested in learning more about Ashley. The proceedings hadn't started yet, and all the rows in the gallery were empty except for the one in the back. Two women were sitting there, both pretty and somewhere between five and ten years older than I was. One was dressed in a business casual, Ann Taylor sort of way, and the other was in a short dress and boots with light blond hair and lots of eyeliner. They were both typing on laptops.

I edge into their row and take out my own computer. It still amazes me that there was Wi-Fi in these courtrooms. The fact that someone could be live-tweeting this sort of thing disturbs me—shouldn't we have been made to sign some sort of nondisclosure agreement?

I'm toggling between Facebook and my work email when I hear someone addressing me from the right side. "Who are you writing for?" asks the blond as I turn to look at her. The other woman stays occupied with her phone. The blond's voice sounds curious and friendly, not competitive, but it is still a bit jarring to be spoken to.

A courtroom lesson that somehow wasn't obvious to me at the outset: people can see you. It might seem ridiculous to point out, but often with the whole theater/stage/audience vibe of the room you really can forget that you're not actually at a play since most of the time everyone is looking straight ahead and you're not making conversation. The bailiff-judge banter is the coming attractions and the oaths are the turn-off-your-cell-phone warnings, and then the show starts—it's amazing that no one has thought to sell popcorn. Most of the time you feel pretty anonymous in a bureaucratic way, like at the DMV. And if you're in and out only once, for the most part you can stay that way.

The people next to you can see you, however. So can the judge and the lawyers and even the defendant. You don't put on a cloak of invisibility when you go inside. It only feels that way, but actually everyone—lawyers especially—is taking note of everyone else. What are you doing there? What is your deal? Might you know something that we could use, or are you someone we should pay attention to? Are you going to make a scene? Are you going to inflame things in the media? If you come back more than one day or even return after the lunch break on the same day, you can't escape having to answer for yourself, I was learning.

The court, I had begun to realize, was the place that was forcing me to get my story straight. I wasn't a journalist—though I played one on TV or, um, was one in my day job—but my presence here was about something else. It was personal and self-motivated and, I feared, a little hard to translate. I was here because Ashley had meant something to me in childhood, even though our relationship as young adults had been more complicated. I was here because even though Ashley hadn't been family, I had a sense that our friendship had almost imprinted something on my DNA. The way I saw myself now was connected to the times we'd had together as kids, and it was that kid I was paying my respects to. It was that kid, that girl, that not-yet-a-woman person, about whom I wanted to know: What happened?

"Um, I'm not writing for anyone. I'm a childhood friend of Ashley's." I say it tentatively, a bit warily, wondering if I should give up the truth so readily. I second- and third-guessed almost all my decisions about Ashley these days. "What about you." That part comes out less like a question and more like a thing to say because I'm already talking and I don't know how to stop and I don't really want to answer any more questions about myself.

"Oh, wow. Okay. I'm from *LA Weekly*," she says. "I'd love to take you to coffee at the break. It'd be great to learn more about Ashley and ask you a few things if you're interested." She says this all casually too, like, oh, it's no big deal, we're just two people interested in the same dead girl and how about we go get lattes and talk it out? Or is this just what real journalists were always like?

This is something I haven't considered at all. Here I am, just trying to keep my own shit together. I've dropped myself as an observer into a terribly serious, high-stakes situation, the likes of which I've seen only in movies, and my priority at the moment is just to get through the day without getting kicked out or offending anyone in the process. And now a reporter potentially wants to make me part of her story?

But maybe I need something from her, too. She probably already has a file full of things I haven't even thought of yet. She knows how this stuff goes down: how to ask questions, what to look for, which boxes to check. I should be asking her to coffee.

But if I do talk to her—should I talk to her?—how will that look to Jen and Chris and Detective Small? Would that mean I would be playing both sides and if I gave it a try would it make me an asshole? *What would Ashley have wanted?*

"I'm not sure," I murmur, looking down at my screen. "I have some work to do, maybe later. I need to . . ." I trail off.

"Yes, yes, of course," says the blond, who I learn is named Christine. She passes me her card and turns back to her notes. She's fine with it all, has seen this before. Her vibe is confident and experienced. She just asks questions and handles whatever answers come back. It's good. She isn't worried about getting kicked out or offending anyone, she knows what she's doing. I want to project her kind of objectivity and coolness.

After Christine seems suitably ensconced in her computer, I google her. I learn she is a something of a pro on the LA homicide beat. Things like gang shoot-outs, drive-bys, and armed robberies are her stock-in-trade: this woman is the real deal. Her investigative reporting played a crucial part in the identification of a serial killer she named the Grim Sleeper, a man who appeared to have been connected to ten murders of women in South Los Angeles between 1988 and 2007. She got to name a serial killer. I'm impressed and intimidated.

But then in the next moment I'm confused all over again. Wait, what?

She's here for this, too? Even though I've had nine years to get used to news stories about this case, I still haven't fully processed the fact that Ashley's death is a matter of public interest. Not to mention that the major players in this world, this city—a defense attorney from the Dream Team; a reporter who broke serial-killer stories; a bona fide celebrity, Ashton Kutcher—are all part of this thing. Blown-up pictures from our childhood are now in magazines for people to stare at. Media people are taking notes on the mundane details of Ashley's postadolescent years. From two girls playing in the New Jersey woods to two women in a courtroom in Los Angeles—one pale and one a ghost. When will that ever stop feeling so discombobulating?

Pictures of Ashley are being flashed on a projector screen throughout people's testimony. It's the same couple of fun-loving group shots from a party that apparently took place at her house only about a week before the murder. Lindner and Deputy District Attorney Marna Miller are asking all the witnesses if they were there—everyone was, it sounds like.

I don't remember seeing this DA at the continuance last year, but it might have been because things were happening so fast and I didn't know where to look. Miller looks intense and harried and at the ready with her opinions and objections. She's attractive but understated, wearing minimal makeup and a plain pantsuit, a slim jacket hitting right at the end of her hips.

About the party, most of the witnesses say they were there. But who else was there? How about the defendant? What did he do during the party? What was everyone drinking, and how much? Do you recognize this outfit that Ashley's wearing in the snap where she's holding court in the middle of a big group? Most of them do.

I don't. It's not something I could ever imagine wearing, either. It's a gamine-gone-late-nineties look: an off-white sleeveless mock turtleneck and off-white arm warmer–type things. I can't see the bottom, but I'm guessing it's some minidress sort of thing and her shoes are white stiletto heels. It's a strange ensemble when you break it down, but on her it works. Her eyebrows are plucked thin, and her hair is light with a skinny headband and a white flower tucked behind her ear. She's smiling in a delighted way—they all are—except for the guy on the right in the caramel leather jacket. He just looks stoned and a bit smug. There are Justin and Jen, whom I recognize, plus the caramel-jacket guy and two other guys I don't know. Everyone's got their arms around each other and they all have the whitest teeth, so straight and so even, like an ad for some whitening gum or a movie poster for a rom com about the good old days. They are clearly the good old days, the glory days, the days of wine and roses—or coke and synthetic hair flowers, depending on whom you asked.

I look at that picture for a while, and I think about how much Ashley liked the camera. The posing we would do, the photo shoots and the scenes and the make-believe in our bedrooms or in the woods. Playing characters, playing at being grown up, playing at making each other laugh—we'd switch in and out by the minute. However the pictures came out, whenever they came out, was never the point—often we wouldn't even look at them again. They'd end up in a box or in a drawer or sometimes still in their paper sleeve from the photo place. The recording of the moments was the fun part, the extra sense of importance it would convey to things. With every click, every roll of film, we were showing each other we were worth remembering.

Over time I'd come to learn a lot from Ashley's friends about her life in LA in the year before she died, and her story was the stuff of Hollywood fantasy—most of it, at least. She had just turned twenty-two, and it felt as though she were in the midst of a never-ending sweet spot. Things just seemed to happen to her in Los Angeles—good things, magical things,

things that made her feel alive, chosen. She could be walking down the street, and someone would stop her, compliment her, and invite her to a premiere. She could be in a shoe store and the manager would decide to bring out this one amazing pair of heels that some actress had forgotten to pick up, and they would fit her perfectly. She could be in a restaurant and her meal would be comped, for no reason at all except that someone had noticed her and liked what he saw.

The weekends in Vegas gave her more money than she knew what to do with. She leased a maroon BMW to get around town, and though she had, technically, transferred to the Fashion Institute of Design & Merchandising, there was just too much stuff going on that she'd rather do than be in class. Parties, clubs, guys, all of it. What was the point of school—of working at something boring on account of the future—when the present was so fantastic? When Justin decided to move down from San Francisco, it seemed like the perfect time to get a new place.

Ashley and Justin had met at a rave in San Francisco back in high school. They'd hooked up once at eighteen, but it had been just a random party thing. No drama, no hard feelings. Justin was gay now, but he and Ashley still sometimes liked to act like a couple for fun. The two of them had known each other longer than any of Ashley's other friends in LA, which meant a lot to her. He felt like family.

They found a sweet little bungalow in the Hollywood Hills: 1911 Pinehurst Road, modest, pale yellow with a driveway, a dog park across the street, and a very cute property manager, Mark Durbin, thrown in free of charge. Later, Jen would move into Justin's room after he left to live with his new guy, but before all that there were parties to be had, as many as they could: small ones every other week or so, and then there was that one from the court photos where they packed almost a hundred people inside. It was as though the place had an open-door policy—their circle just kept on growing. *Sure! Come on by! Why not? Someone is always around*. They collected friends the way regular people picked up lint on sweaters.

No one knew much about what went on when Ashley went to Vegas, however, and they didn't want to ask questions. It felt easier not to know. When Ashley returned from those weekends away, it was almost like she was in a funk; she'd be tired and withdrawn and not up for doing much outside the house. They knew to give her space for a few days until she was back to her old self. Chris would tell me later that he was never sure whether it was about coming down off drugs or feeling horrible about what she had just done in Vegas or whatever had happened to give her so much goddamn cash—he didn't pry. He knew she wasn't proud of it, and the two of them were more about the good times. They never talked about anything that might get in the way.

I could relate. It was a slippery slope, knowing too much. You might start to get too emotionally involved, and then you'd worry when she wasn't around, and then if you brought it up you might come off as judgmental. You might feel responsible, then, and feeling responsible always ended badly. Don't ask, don't tell was the only choice, really. That way, you could pretend it wasn't really happening.

Your twenties were funny like that, I saw from the rearview mirror, now thirty-one. Back then that adulthood thing had still been so new! You could drive and drink and fuck whomever you wanted, but none of it really counted toward your final grade, right? There would still be plenty of time to become who you were supposed to be. It didn't need to happen right this minute. Sure, what's-her-name was rail thin from all the speed and still puked up her food whenever she remembered to eat, but she'd get it together eventually. And yeah, it was true, that guy was a total shit when it came to women, no way would you want him around your friends, but he'd straighten out when he met a girl who could handle him. This was not the moment for reckonings. Those could totally come later, and, hell, by then it would probably be someone else's problem.

If they were crafty, though, people showed you only what they wanted you to see, and it didn't occur to you that perhaps what they didn't want you to see was the important stuff. You had habits, too, that maybe weren't the most healthy or kind. You had different versions of yourself that came out in different situations, and then you had the one you were when you were all alone or in a place where you didn't have to be accountable. The you that ate peanut butter from the jar while sitting on your couch in yesterday's underwear or the you that accidentally ran over that stray cat and kept on driving. The you that stole the painkillers your girlfriend got after her root canal and swallowed them all over two days after telling her you didn't know where they were or the you that did lines off the back of the toilet in that basement club in Berlin and then maybe pretended you had blacked out the rest of the night so you didn't have to face the guy you let jerk off in front of you while your eyes grew heavy. You didn't know it yet, but you were becoming yourself. The behaviors you were developing now would end up being the ones that defined you if you weren't careful.

Gargiulo sits next to Lindner, wearing the same baggy orange jumpsuit I last saw him in and looking even thinner than before. On his back it says LA COUNTY JAIL XXX in black block letters like some twisted sports jersey logo. His skin looks rough and his head is shaved, and he almost resembles a cancer patient or else someone much, much older. He has a weird goatee. He's only a few years older than we are—I mean I am, I have to keep reminding myself. He's fidgety and muttering to himself, occasionally trying to get his attorney's attention in the middle of a sentence to argue with something that's being said or a line of questioning happening in real time, like a person who talks over you when you're in an argument and things are getting heated. Lindner is clearly frustrated but tries not to break his concentration. I can't pick out the words from where I'm sitting, but the energy is there.

On the subject of energy, I've gradually adjusting to the feeling of being in the same room with him, the defendant. Mr. Gargiulo. That guy. *The* guy. The first time it happened last year, the whole thing went by so quickly, I didn't have time to register a vibe. Now I've had hours of sitting here to take it all in, the idea that we're both occupying space in the same confined area. The years and the actions and the sequence of events have brought us here for completely different reasons, but still, we both knew her. Our breath molecules are probably mingling together somewhere in the middle of the room, hovering above everything that's going on before floating up to burn away against the buzzing fluorescent lightbulbs.

When there's a lull in the goings-on, I watch the side of his face, reading his lips. I size up his jawline, his hairline, his slumped posture: I'm a few feet away from the guy who killed Ashley. What the fucking fuck. And then sometimes: Is this really the guy who killed Ashley? How can we really know for sure with no DNA match and no witnesses? What's he thinking right now? What must it be like to be trapped in this never-ending cycle of being in and out of a room where your life is on the line? Why does he look so unconcerned? And then some moments I'd wonder if I was a horrible person even to consider his perspective at all. Who does that? Does that make me unsympathetic? A bad friend? A bad person? A few times Gargiulo turns toward the gallery and we almost make eye contact, but I quickly avert my eyes. What do I think will happen if we actually exchange a glance?

Jen starts to answer the party-girl, question, and District Attorney Miller surprisingly doesn't interject. Most of the questions from Lindner are met by a swift objection from Ms. Miller. I'm glad she's a woman. I have quickly bestowed upon her herolike status as a crusader for justice and female victims' rights, but that's not hard to do when the defense seems determined to portray Ashley as a reckless, coke-snorting whore.

"In fact, Miss Ellerin slept with her landlord. . . . Do you know if he had keys?"

(This is news to me.)

"At any time while you were in the house, were there any male visitors in her bedroom that you saw?"

"I'm going to object as vague and ambiguous as to time," says Miller. The judge asks for clarification.

Other versions of the question showed up later with Chris. "Did Miss Ellerin have a reputation as being sexually available to men?"

"Objection! A reputation?"

"Sustained."

"Do you have an opinion?"

"Objection!"

"Sustained."

It goes on like this for some time, Lindner pushes the envelope with most people from Ashley's crowd only to be shot down by Miller, rinse, repeat. How many ways are there to pretend not to be asking if Ashley was a slut? What does that even mean, anyway? If we were in the Victorian era, we might ask: "Was she a loose woman, the kind you'd turn your head from if you passed her on the street?" If we were in the fifties, perhaps: "Would she be the type your mother would warn you against?" If it were the sixties, maybe we'd call her a free-love counterculture type. But if we could be straight up, we might just ask, "Did she have a lot of sex? And does that justify her murder?" It's unfortunate that the easiest way might be to say it just like that, but all the talking around the issues has the effect of making it sound much nastier, scarlet letter–ish, town square public-stoning style. I'm taking notes through all of this, and my fingers are flying over the keys, transcribing phrases and questions verbatim that sound straight out of a dark thriller. Drugs, sex, adultery—and we're only into the first few hours of the first day.

I had no idea everything would be happening this quickly and this aggressively. I had no idea there would even be so much focus on Ashley—I had assumed I'd be hearing a lot about the other victims, too. I'm learning stories about Ashley's life that I was only able to speculate about, and the truth is crazier than anything I thought up on my own. It's like every stereotype of the good girl gone bad, the ingenue eaten up by the great big seductive, manipulative, unforgiving city of Los Angeles. How much of this is accurate, and how much is the defense's fault? Am I just hooking on to Lindner's ideas because he's adding more zing? And in that case, will a jury do the same?

I assumed there would at least be some kernel of familiarity in the person being described up there, some hint of recognition of the Ashley I knew or even the one I had spent time with a decade ago that week in New York. She was jaded and cynical and way more experienced than I was, but she was also curious about me and thoughtful and excited about things other than drugs. What about piano? Or, I don't know, helping her neighbors or stuff about school? Was there any of that? Instead, all this has me picturing a truly hardened, reckless person who I'm not sure I ever would have spent time with or even crossed paths with, for that matter. She was sleeping with her landlord on the same day she had a date with Ashton Kutcher? She did crack? She was out of my orbit in every sense.

I hate that feeling, and even worse than that, I know that the defense is doing a good job in picking at the state's case. Since we're just at the preliminary hearing phase, the state's burden is only to prove probable cause that the defendant committed the murder. During the trial, they will have to prove it beyond a reasonable doubt. I can imagine how the defense might just line up the details of Ashley's comings and goings and attempt to reduce her to a careless, risk-taking, unflattering trope. It's incredibly hard to hear and feels deeply unfair, but I get it. Both of the attorneys are just doing what they're supposed to be doing, and who knows who really believes what. Can there be a reasonable doubt that the defendant, Michael Gargiulo, actually did it? Couldn't it have been any number of people, 'cause, hell, this girl barely closed the door to her house, let alone her legs? Objection! Sustained! And on it goes. All of that doesn't change the fact that Ashley was murdered or suggest that she deserved to be, but still. Just putting it out there, folks. You can draw your own conclusions.

It was just a few hours into testimony, but it was already easy to pick out the competing narratives the two sides were throwing down about Ashley. Marna Miller mostly stuck to the facts; she called witnesses to speak about the crime scene and some background witnesses who told anecdotes of Gargiulo's creepiness. One woman alluded to an incident that couldn't be discussed on the record, and another who lived in his apartment building said he had once put a knife to her throat. "He asked if I know how to defend myself in case somebody ever held a knife to my throat," she recounted on the stand, saying that Gargiulo had asked her that one day out of the blue. She stayed calm as she said it, not looking at him. The story continued chillingly: she had said no, and then he had come up behind her and done it. She had stayed frozen with fear, she said, and then he had just laughed. Christ.

I learned that Ashton Kutcher had been excused from the preliminary hearing for some reason, but his statement was read by Detective Thomas Chevolek. It was brief and contained nothing I hadn't already learned from *InTouch* and others: he and Ashley had plans that night to meet for drinks around 10:30 p.m. He was going to the house of someone named Christy to watch the Grammys but told Ashley they'd hook up after. He called her three times that day. She called him at 8:24 p.m. He called her back. There was a lot of calling. When he got to Ashley's house around 10:45 p.m., the lights were on and her maroon BMW was parked in the driveway. Ashton knocked on the door several times, looked in the window, and saw what he thought was red wine on the carpet to her bedroom. He left, figuring she had blown him off.

Marna Miller also placed Gargiulo at the scene prior to the night of the murder through testimony about all the times he had stopped by Ashley's house unannounced after the two of them had met on the street when he'd helped Chris change a flat tire, the day that had started it all. Chris, then a fashion stylist, now a hairstylist, had showed up one afternoon after a photo shoot, as he did most days, and parked in front of Ashley's house to pick her up to go out for lunch or coffee or tanning, one of those things they always did together. When they'd come out a few minutes later, the car's back tire was mysteriously flat. Chris had gotten down on the ground and begun checking it out, and Ashley had just laughed. Did he really know how to change a tire? He did and was about to begin doing so when suddenly Gargiulo had appeared, walking down the hill toward them. At the top of the hill was a dead end. Where was he coming from?

Later, Chris would tell me that when he took his tire in to be repaired, the auto shop told him it wasn't actually a regular flat—it had been slashed.

Lindner, for his part, was cross-examining witnesses about the number of parties Ashley had had at the house, introducing the suggestion that Gargiulo and Ashley might have been more than friends and asking for details about her drug use, stripping, and apparently very active sex life. He pushed the boundaries in a big, cringe-making way, and it didn't seem to matter when he got overruled. Lindner only needed his questions to be on the record, and even if the witness didn't end up having to answer, eventually, the jury would be listening.

A few months back I had begun reading the comments online from stories about the case. Most were benign or garden-variety crazy— I worked at a website; I had an intimate understanding of online commenter crazy—but a few felt more threateningly pointed. One from a message board for unsolved crime geeks connected to the A&E *Cold Case Files* show struck me as particularly gross. When I came upon it, I instinctively shook my head like a scolding librarian. Then I cut and pasted the lines into a Word document and hit save:

> This chick was a one-woman Boneathon. A good defense attorney should be able to raise plenty of reasonable doubt due to the "carefree" way she lived her life.

Why did I want a record of that line? I wasn't sure, except that it seemed to underscore the sad fact that Ashley's life no longer belonged to her in an especially cruel manner. It made my protective impulses flare up in a new way. Ashley didn't deserve any of this. She had suddenly been made a public figure for the worst possible reason, and she wasn't around to defend herself or do anything at all, really. She was now being talked about on message boards and in tabloids and in courtrooms by attorneys who had never even met her, and there was nothing anyone could do about it. They could call her whatever they wanted in an open court, and all that could be said was "Objection!" Not to mention, so what if she *had* slept with lots of guys? Did that make her less entitled to live her life without getting murdered? Did that make the loss of her less painful for her friends and family?

And here I was, watching it all play out in front of me in real time just as the Internet troll had said it would: a good defense attorney, a chick being described as a Boneathon, reasonable doubt creeping in: check, check, check—and we weren't even at the real trial yet.

When the judge finally pauses things for lunch, I am more than ready for a break. Christine and the two other media people—one other woman from CBS News arrived later—rush up to the bar behind DA Marna Miller to introduce themselves. I follow them, idly, because it seems like the thing to do. She's gathering her papers together and not looking up when Christine gets her attention. She asks her if she can get her card, and in response Ms. Miller is terse. She sighs and looks up at the lot of us; it feels as if she'd prefer not to deal with us. We stand facing her in a row expectantly, and she goes down the line. "Who are you writing for?" "Who are you writing for?" she asks. *LA Weekly*, CBS News, NBC come the answers. Christine asks if she has time to talk later, and Ms. Miller says probably not. Then it's my turn. "Who are you writing for?" she asks, barely looking up.

I have been asked this before, so this time I am a tiny bit less nervous, though I'm worried she might be confused as to why I'm hanging with the press crowd. It's true I'm an editor, and the thought has crossed my mind that one day maybe I'd write about some of this, somehow. At this moment, though, I have no idea what form it will take and if or when it will ever happen. I want to be transparent, but this feels like too much to explain. "I'm not on assignment," I say. "I'm Ashley's childhood friend." Ms. Miller looks up. She makes eye contact with me. She puts her hand on my shoulder and cocks her head to the side. The transformation is striking.

"I'm so sorry," she says. "If you need anything at all or would like to talk about what's going on, please let me know." Then she hands me her card. I thank her, and we chat for a moment longer—How long am I in town? Where am I from?—as she gathers her things. I feel a surge of connection with DA Miller. I feel her graciousness and her civic duty, and I imagine what it would be like to be her friend. She'd be harried and late for drinks most of the time, but when she finally arrived you'd instantly forgive her. You'd give her a gift certificate for a massage on her birthday, and she'd never get around to using it. She cares. She struggles. She exhibits grace. She fights the good fight.

When I look behind me, all of the other press people are gone. I feel a small bit of guilt about what feels like special treatment from Ms. Miller, the immediate trust she's placed in me and the elevated status that comes with it, no questions asked. Do I deserve it? Am I an imposter? Am I one of them, or am I one of the others?

The DA and I walk out of the courtroom together, and there's Christine, chatting with the CBS woman in the hall outside. They're standing close together, but the two of them catch my eye as we pass and give me a "Well, look at you, missy" nod. I smile wanly.

In the afternoon it's Chris's turn on the stand. Watching him up there is the most wrenching yet—he's the most emotional of anyone who's testified so far. He's teary and choked-up almost from the get-go, and I feel for him, even as my cynical side questions the display. It's almost histrionic—isn't this a little excessive for a person you knew only eight months? It's also been nine years since. Was it really possible to get that close in such a short time and for the wound to be still so open?

But as I got to know Chris over the coming years, I'd grow to understand more about what this was really all about, where the tears were coming from and where they often headed to, and how the way a person carries loss with him can be as individual as a fingerprint.

I'd learn that Chris came on the scene through Justin. They had first connected online in an AOL gay chat room and had even hooked up a few times, but Justin had said he lived with his girlfriend. Weird, but whatever, man, not my business, Chris had thought. Once, Justin invited Chris over to the house when Ashley was home and suggested that the three of them go out together. Chris was confused. Why would he want to go out with his hookup partner and that guy's girlfriend?

Right away, Chris and Ashley hit it off, and that put him into a tricky position. Finally he just went for it. "I don't know how to tell you this," he told Ashley, "but your boyfriend's gay." Ashley got a kick out of that one and assured Chris that she and Justin were just friends. "Good, 'cause you didn't seem that stupid," Chris said.

After that they were inseparable. Breakfast, lunch, coffee, drinks, tanning. They both ran in a young celebrity crowd, so they already knew a lot of people in common. They saw each other just about every day and were always getting into something. Chris spent the night there a lot, too. In Justin's bed, in Ashley's bed, on the couch—he treated it like a second home. He and Ashley had similar attitudes about drugs, too—a passing interest in coke and crystal, mostly. It could be fun if it was around, but it wasn't really their style to get strung out. Every so often they'd agree that they needed to take it easy, but they were never too worried about it.

The same went for men. For Ashley, they were everywhere, and they wouldn't let up! Chris told me he couldn't believe how much male attention she attracted, wherever they went and no matter what she was wearing. People were always asking if she was an actress, and then it would start from there. Rich dudes, models, Hollywood types—they all sort of blurred together.

I could easily picture what he meant; I had seen it myself when Ashley and I had gone out in New York, how captivated and shameless the guys were. I wondered how it felt to Chris, a gay man, to observe it all at the time. To me, a straight woman, I remembered it feeling brutal. Seeing the way men looked at Ashley to me felt like power, power I had felt outside of.

In the years since, my feelings had shifted; the male gaze felt like power only up to a point; it could just as easily be disempowering. Sure, it was fun to flirt when someone cute noticed you, but how about when your boss looks inappropriately at your chest during a meeting? How about when you're walking home alone and there's someone following you? Or how about, God forbid, a serial killer moves in down the road and you happen to catch his eye?

Harnessing male desire in and of itself would always be a losing game and potentially a dangerous one, as men would always have the upper hand. Playing the game might open a few doors, it might lead to some fleeting excitement, but it wasn't the path to a deeper fulfillment or even a good relationship. It had taken me most of my twenties—a time in which I gradually came into a sense of sexual confidence I imagined Ashley had felt early on—to figure that out. Sexual power didn't lead to happiness or fulfilling relationships with men. That sort of confidence, that sort of groundedness, was about something much more hard won than the right makeup and heels.

My understanding of my last memories of Ashley had changed, too. Now I see that that last weekend in New York, it only looked as though she had all the power she could ever need. There was a whole other world waiting for her that she didn't get a chance to access. I can see now that Ashley might have been just at the moment of starting to get bored with it all. That was why the episode with Oliver was so disappointing; she had hoped that it might have been a glimpse into the other side. At twenty-one, she was pushing up against the limits of what sex could make possible, and part of her was yearning to be on to the next thing. What might it have been for her?

• • •

"What kind of girl was Ashley Ellerin?" Lindner asks Chris.

"Beautiful. Fun. Outgoing. Friendly." Chris begins to cry. The air in the room is heavy and sad; it feels as if there's a storm outside even though it's still the same brilliantly sunny LA day it always is. It's as if people are breathing more slowly, as if we're watching a painful medical procedure, one that's necessary and will potentially make the patient's life easier in the long run but in the present it's all needles and scalpels and cries and viscera. I almost feel complicit, getting to sit on this side of things, taking notes, watching it all unfold. Being able to walk out of the room if I want, evade eye contact.

"What kind of crowd did Ashley hang out with?" asks Lindner.

"Some celebrity types, young Hollywood . . ." Chris trails off. Young Hollywood. I picture MTV's *The Hills* or some E! show about children of the stars. Mercedes-Benzes and movie premieres and nightclubs and red carpets and acting like an asshole to the valet.

"This crowd—did they do drugs?"

"Smoking crystal meth, doing cocaine," Chris says with resignation. I wonder if he's embarrassed at all. I wonder if he wishes he could lie—or maybe there are some aspects he's lied about already? He must know this doesn't sound good, that it makes them look like stereotypes, and that they can scarcely afford a drop in sympathy points. But he's also not one to overexplain things it seems, and I respect that.

The questions roll forward: What was her house like? What sort of people stopped by? Were they always announced?

"No."

"Why was it different when [the defendant] stopped by unannounced?" Lindner asks.

"He just wasn't in our group of friends," says Chris.

"It was a question of class, was it?" Lindner persists. "A question of not being a Hollywood guy?" He draws out this last part, almost sneering.

You're all just a bunch of beautiful, seedy trust funders, and my client was an earnest middle-class man and you call him creepy and assume he's a serial killer. You judgy entitled young Hollywood fucker. Or so I hear in the pauses.

Objection! Sustained.

Minutes tick by. Marna Miller takes a turn. Tears. Silence. Crumpled tissues being shoved into pockets. Repetition. The stories and the phrases recur like lyrics and a chorus. Young Hollywood. Beautiful. Flirtatious. He just wasn't in our group of friends.

During the slower parts I google Chris's hair salon. It's a hip-looking place in Pasadena called Crowned Studio Salon with a punk-inspired, accessible website. In the staff bios section, I spot stylists with lip rings and mohawks and purple streaks in their hair. Chris smiles brightly in his head shot. He is the Lead Cutting Specialist.

"Did you find the defendant's behavior threatening?"

Objection! Overruled.

"Did you tell Detective Small that you thought the defendant was acting stalkerish?"

Objection! Sustained.

"After you told [Ashley] about the defendant and that you thought he was stalkerish and weird and strange, did the defendant still show up at the residence . . . and did she still let him in?"

"Yes." Chris's voice cracks, and he grabs for a tissue. Of course yes. Ashley's death is not his fault or her fault, but it's why we're all here watching this horror movie, shouting at the screen "Don't open the door!" a thousand times over, isn't it? Do you have to make him relive it all? Do you have to make *us*?

Finally, mercifully, it's done. Chris leaves the stand slowly, lethargically, depleted, and I can see the relief dripping off him as he walks toward the door even as it's coupled with perhaps some shame. When you're up there testifying, even though it's the victim they're asking about, it's you who's put up on the operating table, I am learning. How you spent your time, decisions you made, all of it is suddenly relevant. You're being picked at just the same, and you're actually alive to face it, and it hurts, and it's not fair, and you can't get out of it. But for now, relief trumps all. Chris is finished. He can get a drink, rejoin his friends, put this all behind him for a bit.

He did his best, I'm sure of it, but I'm left with the uncomfortable sense that something felt a little unrelatable about him, or at least just now. Maybe it's his hair-trigger tears or his tales of drug use. I feel like an asshole for thinking all this, and I feel the urge to run out after him. To find him and console him, to tell him I was there. That I know how hard it was—how hard it is. I know he did what he could. But instead I stay seated, I type notes. I look around at Christine and the CBS woman and the lawyers as if it's all fine. We just witnessed the same stuff, my internal dialogue is the same as theirs, nothing to see here. I tell myself I'm not even sure that that kind of thing would be allowed—he's probably busy with Jen and her boyfriend and Justin in the hallway. I'm too new; what could I say that would even make a difference? It's not clear where I belong yet or whether I'm to be trusted, anyway. Like the defendant, at least for now, I'm just not in their group of friends.

11

SCORPIO RISING

COME AROUND THE curve of Sunset Boulevard a few blocks past Fairfax, and you see Chateau Marmont emerging like some fantasy castle in the sky, all gleaming white spires and faux Gothic arches and Italianate pointy trees reaching up and up. It looks so much like a European estate from the fifteenth century that if you squint your eyes you almost don't notice there's a Starbucks/rental car outfit right down the road and a flashy Mexican place called the Pink Taco across the street.

The Chateau, everyone in LA calls it. "The after party was at the Chateau," says my actress friend, who also does voice-overs. "Let's definitely get drinks at the Chateau when you're in town," says another, in development but technically the assistant to a showrunner. I find all of it—the job titles, the fake-European allusion—laughably pretentious, but I'm just not from around here.

The place has certainly earned its city lore. Built in the 1920s as Los Angeles's first earthquake-proof apartment building, the Chateau quickly became the spot for bad behavior of all types in Golden Age Hollywood and thereafter. Back then, studios had a code of conduct written into stars' contracts for what was permitted on camera as well as what was expected of them in public. Who those people really were was another story, and the studios knew that with or without their control, something would have to give. To make up the difference, the studios rented rooms at the Chateau for stars to go at it and get up to no good. Clark Gable and Jean Harlow were rumored to have had a torrid affair upstairs. Howard Hughes was said to have gawked from his room through binoculars at women around the pool. Led Zeppelin's drummer rode his motorcycle through the lobby. Roman Polanski fled there after his statutory rape charges before leaving the country. John Belushi overdosed in Bungalow Three. Helmut Newton fatally crashed his car in the driveway. Lindsay Lohan holed up there during her first drunk-driving scandal.

The Chateau is like a movie set that way, an intricately constructed fantasy that encourages you to play against type. It's like being in permanent vacation mode. It's a place where you can imagine losing all your clothes, and then maybe your mind, and still wanting to go back as soon as you're able to. It's a place where you can picture getting discovered or meeting someone who might change your life, whether for good or ill you don't yet know but you go ahead with it anyway. And it came as little surprise to me to learn from Chris that this magical mystery castle was Ashley's playground.

Ashley would go to the Chateau with her crowd for late-night drinks at the turn of the millennium, lazing about in the low lighting and faux worn banquettes in the bar, drinking Red Bull and vodkas. Did she ever meet someone and make her way upstairs to a suite or the penthouse? Did she ever skinny-dip in the pool or give anyone a fake-but-real lap dance on a dare? Did she ever do lines in the bathroom with a Spanish director in town for the Golden Globes or the girlfriend of an exec from Paramount? The potentially illicit scenarios were endless.

Marisa and Rainn, my hosts on this trip, have brought me here to-night. It's only a few minutes from their bungalow in West Hollywood, where I'm sleeping on an air mattress in the spare room that Rainn oc-casionally uses as his office. With its Spanish-style roof and front terrace looking out over Laurel Canyon, it's hard to liken the house to anything that exists in Brooklyn because it's one of those completely Californian structures that would be impossible to picture anywhere else, not to men-tion the fact that the person who pays its not insubstantial rent—Marisa's boyfriend, Rainn—makes his living as a lunar astrologer.

Marisa and I have known each other for quite some time, stretching back to my first years out of college in New York, pre-9/11, pre–Ashley's death, pre–a lot of things that would come to leave a permanent mark on us both. Ours had been the kind of friendship that faded in and out for years at a time over petty squabbles that turned into public rows and, finally, quasi referendums on our individual values, which at times seemed to di-verge wildly. We would find our way back together again at the usual cross stations: boyfriends coming and going, apartment leases broken, though we could never keep it up for long. After she had moved to California following a messy breakup, we had achieved the closest thing yet to consis-tency between us. The distance had seemed to soften the edges, lower the stakes—perhaps age had done that, too. We didn't have to have everything in common to love each other—maybe we didn't have to have much at all.

Now we saw each other a few times a year—I'd stay at her place when I visited to research Ashley, and she'd be at mine in Brooklyn when she was back east seeing family. Rainn had been her man since even before she had touched down in Los Angeles, a souvenir from her cross-country journey. Their origin story was distinctly wacky and one I loved to retell to friends. He had been her telephone astrologer on and off throughout her twenties; they'd speak twice a year for hourlong readings of her chart: what to look out for, what planetary alignments would be affecting her, which romantic entanglements were to be avoided, that kind of thing. Marisa was a passionate believer in astrology and would argue for its classification as a science to anyone who dared challenge her. "If our bodies are ninety-three percent water and the earth is seventy-one percent water and the moon and the planets control the oceans, how can we claim we're not also controlled by them?" she would cry, her voice getting higher and shriller. I had long since learned to let that one lie.

Rainn would send a recording of their calls afterward to her in cassette and eventually CD form, and Marisa had kept all of them from the very first, neatly organized in a box under her bed. They had never met in person, but since she was about a due for her biannual reading at the time of her cross-country move, Rainn suggested they meet up where he was based in Arizona as she was passing through. Maybe it was the breakup she was coming off of that made all of it seem heightened, but the chemistry was instant, as she tells it. The first time she saw him she could barely look away; his aura was so intense she felt she could see a glow around him—he was the most magnetic person in the room. She was attracted to his deep spirituality, and he saw in her the embodiment of everything he had ever hoped for in a partner. They got secretly engaged after just a few months. Why secretly? I could never get a handle on that one. I always figured that despite Marisa's distinct lack of skepticism about many things, even she knew that Rainn and their story had a whiff of the absurd—why bother inviting that kind of criticism just yet? A new relationship was fragile enough.

If Rainn can predict when his clients will or won't meet their soul mate, one might ask, shouldn't he have seen something this life-changing on the horizon for himself? "Everyone always asks that," Marisa says, bemused, without ever giving a clear answer.

We sit outside on the garden patio at the Chateau, an impossibly lovely, shaded courtyard just off the restaurant where the waiters sport starched vests and a hamburger is $23. Terry Richardson is curled up on a thread-bare couch in the corner of the lobby as we come in. Our server looks like a soap opera actor or swimmer or both, and I can't help but wonder if he's come straight from a morning on the water in Venice, his designer wet suit stashed in the staff locker room next to the walk-in cooler in the basement.

The three of us order wine and a cheese plate and chat about what's been happening at the hearing, though it's not I who brings it up. My close friends know a bit about what's going on, and I understand that when they ask about things they're genuinely interested as well as trying to be supportive about issues in my life that have no bearing on them, akin to asking after my great-aunt with Alzheimer's or what's been going on at *New York* magazine. But sometimes I really hate having to talk about it, especially in settings like bars or parties or at brunch. Especially brunch. As practiced as I've become at the sound bites, explaining casually to strangers what I couldn't yet understand about the significance of her life to mine at this point, getting into the new and unprocessed details doesn't seem right, nor does shutting down my friends' kind encourage-ment. The drugs and Chris and the slut shaming and the emotions and all the rest don't feel appropriate at this moment either, on this lovely spring evening with surf-god waiters setting down taleggio and fig jam around us, but Marisa has asked, and she cares and she is my host, and I want to be gracious and throw her a bone.

I also don't like having to bring Rainn in on things as if he were someone I felt close to, but such is how it goes with your friends and their partners. Sometimes it can feel challenging and a dash manipulative on the part of your friend, like "Tell us one of your crazy dating stories while we sit here and gasp and add incredulous murmurs and stare at you while holding hands" or "Tell that one about the fascinating/tragic/painful thing that happened to you so my new boyfriend can see how interesting you are and then we all laugh and I get points for having interesting friends." But that's my role in this friendship scene, stone set as hers. Such is coupling. Such is growing up and watching your friends find their person, or their series of persons. Some times are easier than other times. This is not one of the easier times.

Marisa's been encouraging me to bond with Rainn ever since the first time I met him last year, and I've been dutifully giving it my best effort. Rainn is unfailingly kind, rather soft-spoken, and appears to adore Marisa. However he suffers from the not uncommon affliction of taking his work home with him, which in his case means he is practically single-mindedly focused on astrology to the exclusion of almost all other topics. Everything, to him, is seen through the lens of a telescope pointed up at the moon and stars. Though he can handle a few minutes of polite getting-to-know-you talk, you can see his eyes glaze over when the conversation turns to subjects other than the cosmos, which is to say, most of the time. Again and again I find myself struggling to take him seriously, and then I feel like a judgmental asshole. Wouldn't it be easier if I could just take people at face value? Their beliefs are their beliefs and mine are mine, and there is nothing wrong with that. But in my head, of course, I can never quite leave it at that; I am always trying to pick things apart and poke at the holes.

When Marisa and Rainn bicker, Marisa tells me, Rainn rarely addresses the issue at hand. Instead of discussing, say, why he walked out in a huff or missed an important date, he'll simply invoke the planets to justify why things were destined to go down the way they did. Venus was in retrograde that month, that was why their affection was lacking, he might say, and the full moon was in Aquarius, so there was that. It could never be something as basic as "You hurt my feelings" or "I'd like to be having more sex" between them; it was much more likely to be cycles of restriction and delay: Uranus is active, Neptune's clouding judgment so we can't make this decision now anyway, let's pick it up again at the end of this phase.

Last year when I came for a stay, I let Rainn give me a reading at

Marisa's suggestion. He asked for my birth date and place and time and then took a few hours to prepare my chart, which he then consulted on his computer as he spoke while I sat in front of him, reclining on the couch like in some mock therapy session. I have the ability to look at someone and know exactly who they are, he told me, but I suffer from periods of self-doubt. I am entering a phase where I will manifest my destiny, and I am destined to be a person who inspires growth and change in others. Justice will be very important in this life. I nodded encouragingly and even took a few notes, but the whole thing left me with a vaguely empty feeling. Plenty of what he said was empowering and allowed me to stay safe within my bias about parts of myself I already understood, but I had a hard time sucking it all down. How could I differentiate between what was wise and true and what was just a confident person getting high on his own supply? Or maybe there wasn't much of a difference at all.

We're almost done with our first glass of wine, the cheese plate solidly picked over with just a few cornichons and toast points left around the perimeter. Marisa and I are discussing what we want for our second glass—should we switch to cocktails?—and Rainn hasn't spoken for at least fifteen minutes.

"The majority of serial killers have disrupted water signs," he says suddenly, looking more at the potted fig tree as he speaks than at Marisa or me.

"Gargiulo has a Scorpio rising sign, a water Cancer Moon, and Mars opposing his rising," he continues. Rainn is bald, with a perfectly shaped, round head that he shaves nearly every day and large tribal earrings that stretch his earlobes to the size of a half-dollar. I watch as the light reflects off his taut scalp while I figure out what to say next.

"You did his chart?" I ask. I'm genuinely surprised and not a little touched. The whole thing feels surreal, not to mention somewhat confusing. Had Rainn been listening this whole time when I had thought he just looked bored and out of it? I didn't even realize that Rainn knew Ashley's full name, let alone her accused killer's name. Where had he gone to find his birth date and birthplace, and when had he done all of it? And why?

"I've always been really interested in serial killers," he says, now turning to make eye contact with me. Marisa, strangely, looks uninterested and is not really listening. She's clearly heard similar conversations dozens of times and is occupying herself with the cocktail list as Rainn talks.

"Using Eastern astrology, a large percentage of serial killers have a strong relationship to Pisces, Cancer, or Scorpio along with a violently placed Mars. Jeffrey Dahmer, Ted Bundy, and Richard the Night Stalker all had water moons disrupted by the planet Mars," he continues. I'm not sure how to take this information, or even figure out what any of it means. My first instinct is to say "That's fascinating." But is it? It's more as though this scene that I have found myself in is fascinating.

At certain times over the past few years and in certain places—say, in a courtroom in Los Angeles, at a waterfall outside Seattle, and later at a strip club in Las Vegas and a hair salon in Pasadena—I had become aware of the notion that I wouldn't be where I was that very moment if Ashley hadn't died. Having known her, and having taken this path to understand her death, is the closest thing I've come to an out-of-body experience: the floaty sensation of observing the parallel tracks my life could have taken and how a single action long ago has set off a journey that has reverberated for years and will probably stretch on into the future—maybe it will take me to places I can't even conceive of yet, a mountaintop or a foreign graveyard or maybe even a prison cell. And here, sitting in the immaculate courtyard of this iconic Hollywood hotel, politely listening to a lunar astrologer wax on about famous serial killers' astrological charts and realizing that what I consider to be a pseudoscience has some relevance to my life, is one of those times.

"A disrupted water sign indicates a person who has so much emotion that he ends up shutting his emotions off entirely to try to deal with his life,"

Rainn says. Marisa has ordered a drink while Rainn is talking—a mojito—and now she's turned back toward us and is regarding Rainn from the side, almost in the way of coed talk-show hosts bent on maintaining traditional gender roles. "It's funny: you hear serial killers say that they have no emotion at all, but according to astrology, their emotions are so disrupted or disturbed that their crimes are really about finding violent ways to express the emotions that they very much do have. Gargiulo's alignment creates relentless feelings of violence that would be difficult to contain." Restless feelings of violence. I consider this: the way restlessness feels in the body, an ache, a tingling, a buzzy anxious heat. I feel restless myself right now. Restless for meaning. Restless for clarity. Restless to know how it will all turn out.

What do restless feelings of violence feel like? Have I ever had them? My mind jumps to picturing an angry little boy in a sandbox, unable to express himself, so instead he throws first sand, and his shovel, and then his pail. I picture Gargiulo alone in his apartment before any of the killings went down. Would he have been someone to torture dogs? Or cut himself repeatedly? What might it have been like to enter his apartment? Would the energy have scared me, like the way occasionally on dates in my first few years in New York I'd find myself in a guy's apartment and even though he'd be nothing but skinny or bashful or shy or kind, my hackles would every so often rise a little, just with the awareness that I was with a stranger, a strange man, an unknown element—things could turn on a dime, don't you know.

"He's also got Mars in the seventh, which is common for hatred toward females," Rainn says. He's on a roll now. His voice is picking up speed and insistence; he's clearly in his element. And what an unusual element it is. The science is so unprovable, the arguments so circular, as to seem meaningless. I'm wishing Marisa would help me out at this point. I feel rather alone on this raft of astrological serial-killer pseudoinformation and don't really have the appropriate language to respond. I'm afraid of insulting him or sounding too challenging in my questions. She would know what to say, I'm certain. The suspension of disbelief, the way of just listening to someone talk without feeling the need to break it all down and make it a comment on who they are or what it means about you—she'd always been good at that.

Rainn is getting even more excited now, discussing impotence and homosexuality and latent anger, all the dark aspects of Mars in the seventh house. "Imagine all the rage you'd be carrying if you were a rapist who is impotent," he says. Nope, sorry, can't.

I look ahead and see Terry Richardson walk past the open doorway inside, on his way somewhere across the lobby, up, up, and away toward distant lands of eroticism and intrigue. Rainn is a good man, I have decided. A very peculiar one, but good. He is trying to connect in his own way, using the tools he has, using his words as we all do. Don't we all speak different languages from one another, essentially? I feel myself becoming more and more California as I sink deeper into my lounge chair. Rainn's blue is different from my blue and his love is different from my love and how he looks at the moon and stars is entirely different from anything I can conceive of. The best we can hope for is that our individual understandings of the world can mesh somehow, I'm thinking. It all makes so much sense in this exquisite golden light.

I have zoned out a bit now, but he's still talking, and it's okay. The words have become just absurd and repetitive enough to be almost soothing. I catch every other phrase or so: astronomically impossible, Bundy, deep emotion.

I watch the mint curl around the straw of Marisa's mojito that has just arrived, the puckered leaves sticking out of the glass like a tiny fern. I breathe in the scent of the plants at the Chateau: the sickly sweet pink flowers that bloom and dry up and bloom again, the woodsy musk of the old skinny trees that have seen skinny movie stars dance beneath them. The moon is so low, it's almost like it's sitting right here with us.

12

TO BEAR WITNESS

"IF SHE WAS with us today, she would, I feel, be someone important," Justin says with confidence in front of all of us from the stand. His testimony is heavy on feelings and intuitions and dramatic moments of reckoning, yet he displays far less emotion than Chris did and hardly seems nervous at all. He has his story down clearly and he sticks to it, his floppy hair falling over his face occasionally as he speaks. He pushes it aside with his right hand and continues talking. He doesn't tire or tear up—his demeanor actually has more in common with the law enforcement officials who have spoken earlier than with any of Ashley's other friends. Perhaps he's done this before.

Ashley was "a very amazing person that would love to make friends with anyone," he says. Justin's grammar is not very amazing, and I'm having a hard time ignoring his odd word choices and verb misconjugations and mix-ups between that and who and which and whom. I feel guilty for being judgmental, but then a moment later I consider that a potential jury might think the same thing, and then I feel annoyed. This is the prelude to a goddamned capital murder trial for an alleged serial killer, goddammit—every detail counts. Pinstripes, billboard business, misplaced modifiers—you're sending out signifiers whether you realize it or not. If there were ever a time for precision, surely it is now.

Despite his diction, Justin's account is eerie and compelling, and he paints himself as someone with a sixth sense for danger. It's hard not to wonder how much of this is 20/20 hindsight or the massaging of details through years of repetition, but nonetheless enough facts and anecdotes are in place that I'm experiencing a bit of a horror movie heightened anxiety state while listening to him.

Ashley and Justin had just moved to the Pinehurst bungalow when Gargiulo entered the picture, Justin explains.

"Would it be a fair statement to say that Ashley became involved with a number of men while you lived with her?"

"Objection!"

"Sustained."

There's that old nugget again. Same question, different words, different person on the stand. Or are they the same words? Is it still the same person up there? I can't recall, and it hardly matters at this point, anyway; it's all blurring together. I have become inured to the fact that nearly every witness who knew Ashley will be asked, early on, some version of a casual query in disguise by the defense, forcing the witness to catalogue Ashley's sex life, drug use, and promiscuity. Most questions will prompt sustained objections, though some won't. And then we'll get on with things. If only they could get it out of the way in the beginning: "State your name. Relationship to the victim. How would you rate her on the sluttiness scale? Six? OK, good. Moving on."

Justin never really felt settled into the house, he continues, and moved out after a few months because he "didn't have a good feeling about [the place]." Later, Chris would pull in his friend Jen to take over the lease as Ashley's new roommate, but before all that happened, a bunch of peculiar—to me it sounded downright terrifying—stuff went down.

First was the time Justin was tasked with driving Gargiulo home from an art gallery opening they were at a short while after they met him. All of them were a little weirded out by the guy, but somehow Justin had gotten stuck taking him out one night. Gargiulo was over at the house, looking into their broken heater, and asked if he could tag along to the opening, so Justin felt sort of obligated, seeing as he was helping them. On the way back, there came a moment in the car when Gargiulo put his hand on top of Justin's on the stick shift. "He grabbed my hand," Justin acts out, using the open palm of his left hand to cover the fist of his right. It makes a dull clapping sound.

The gesture freaked Justin out, to the point that he immediately wanted Gargiulo out of the car. Justin is gay. Was Gargiulo hitting on him? Miller asks. Justin says no. He says all this quite steadily, as if he's reading from a book but with a dash of "Can you believe it?" thrown in. There are none of the pauses or shaky voice of the rest of the friends who have testified. Not that I'm enjoying seeing people stutter and shake up there, but Justin's affect does feel like a bit of a disconnect, especially considering that the narrative he's telling is one of the most dramatic ones we've heard so far.

He continues: Later that same night, Justin was walking home from a friend's house and saw Gargiulo's green truck parked across the street from his and Ashley's house. It was 3 a.m. He knew it was the truck because of the dangly wicker cross Gargiulo had hanging from the rearview mirror. Justin had seen it before. The whole thing raised a red flag. He immediately went inside and got on the phone to call Ashley, who was out. "This isn't, you know, normal," he said he remembered thinking. He tried to call her over and over again, but couldn't reach her.

The next morning, almost as soon as Justin opened his eyes, the phone rang. It was Gargiulo; he wanted to come in right away and see what parts he needed to get to fix the heater.

Chris would tell me later that the timing of things was a little too convenient: Ashley's house was always cold, so they liked to keep the heat on, and then suddenly her heater broke, right after Chris and Ashley had met Gargiulo. Right after he had given them his card, right after he had helped with Chris's flat tire, and right after he'd said he was a heating and air-conditioning man. How funny that the next day, when the furnace conked out, they had just met someone they could call?

Gargiulo came in that morning, and Justin asked what he had been doing outside in the middle of the night. He started stuttering, Justin says. He seemed to be caught off guard. "I can't go home," he said. The FBI was there trying to get his DNA because his best friend's girlfriend had been murdered.

"If you're innocent, you have nothing to hide," Justin says he told him.

With that, Gargiulo put his foot up on the couch, as Justin tells it, and then he raised his pant leg to reveal a knife in a case strapped to his calf. Gargiulo pulled out the knife to show Justin. What happened next? That line of questioning progresses into a discussion of how big the knife was, and then Justin says he rushed Gargiulo out of the house. "I told him I didn't want to have anything to do with this business."

After that, Miller pivots the questioning to parties, and we never really learn what happened next, at least what happened next that moment. Ostensibly their heater got fixed, parties were planned, and a few months later Ashley was dead. There was no shouting or fisticuffs or any of the disturbed reactions that to me would feel appropriate just then, though Justin did finally get a hold of Ashley to tell her what happened. The morning unfolded: showers were taken, coffee was brewed. Is it me, or is everyone in California just way more chill with weirdness, danger, and risk? Is it the drug use? The sunshine? Is it something in the water?

Justin admits that he thought Gargiulo was a creep and that he told Ashley that, but not in any particularly alarming way. There was no "Ashley, you're in danger, girl." Or even "Get away from this guy, he's trouble." More just like, "Eh, that guy. Do you have to invite him to our next party?" Ugh. Okay. Fine.

Justin did copy down Gargiulo's license plate number that morning and sent it to his mother's private detective. But then a few weeks later when Gargiulo stopped by again unannounced and Ashley was out of town, Justin still let him in to join a small preholiday gathering he was having. "Why?" asked Miller.

"I let him in because I wanted him to feel that what he said to me . . . I wanted to show that I really didn't care about it, so there wouldn't be any problem thereafter."

But that knife! That knife! I wanted to shout. Who carries a concealed weapon like that? Who carries a concealed weapon and tells stories about being pursued by the FBI in connection to a murder and then still gets invited to parties? I was flummoxed, truly. Was the knife somehow passed off as related to his HVAC work? Was he so good-looking that none of this mattered? Did he just seem crazy but harmlessly so, not to be taken too seriously? Is it too easy to assume now that if anyone I had just met revealed a concealed knife to me in my home I would be terrified and immediately call the police? Or maybe that's just because I look at knives differently now.

"Did you ever tell the defendant that Ashley was a stripper?" Deputy District Attorney Miller asks.

"No," Justin answers swiftly. It's clear that everyone wishes that this stripping stuff would just go away—it's not relevant to the Ashley they knew, it's not relevant to her death—but of course it won't. More questions roll out, more calls for speculation about what really happened to Ashley in Vegas and why she kept going.

"Was it your belief that she needed the lifestyle if she didn't need the money?" Lindner asks later.

"She was a party girl," Justin replies, as if that explained it all.

There was that phrase again: party girl. Jen was asked about it, and now Justin answers with it. What does it really mean? There seem to be a few different definitions. In a generous reading, it could be synonymous with fun-loving, but in this hearing it is being used as a catchall euphemism. There is also a crucial distinction between being "the life of the party" and a party girl, and, depending on the context, that distinction seems to contain some gendered judgment. A young woman who enjoys a good party is fine—perhaps she liked to drink a little too much, but for the most part she's fun to have around and doesn't offend anyone. A party girl, on the other hand, seems to suggest promiscuity and perhaps something a little predatory and desperate. A party girl may be unsafe. A party girl may be "asking for it." A party girl isn't connected to any one man. A party girl isn't your mother or your sister, and she's definitely not your wife. A party girl is escapist, a party girl burns bridges, a party girl isn't too concerned with exactly whom she parties with, as long as the party stays fun.

Where did Ashley's brand of party girl fit into all that? Years later, I would find myself in Las Vegas for the first time, visiting the club where Ashley had worked in hopes of figuring out more.

The DA after Marna Miller gave me the name—Cheetah's—and suggested that beautiful LA women flying to Sin City on Friday evenings for weekends of light sex work—stripping, escorting, whatever—wasn't as unusual as it sounded. "Go to Burbank airport on a Friday night, and they're everywhere," he said. It didn't have to have deep psychological implications, he said, and for many girls the money was just too good to pass up.

I wanted to see for myself.

I took the night off from a media conference I was attending in downtown Vegas and headed over in a cab after dinner, a few new friends from the program in tow. After I'd mentioned my agenda for the evening earlier that day to my assigned roommate—"I'm planning on visiting the strip club where my murdered friend worked more than a decade ago"— by the afternoon, word had spread through the group, and suddenly I had scores of volunteers offering to accompany me. I was grateful for the moral support and even a little bit touched, even though I imagined that for them the whole thing was probably just a voyeuristic lark, fodder for the stories they could tell back home.

I had been to only one strip club before—a very soft-core place in the New York Financial District that also hosted rock shows—and I didn't consider myself someone who would visit one unironically unless I had a very good reason. This was clearly a good reason, though I still wanted to get in and out as soon as possible. My goal was to just get a look at the place, to see if I could picture Ashley there, to soak in how it felt to be inside.

The club was a grungy, trashily hip spot in a desolate area on Western about fifteen minutes off the strip, the kind of place you probably wouldn't wander into on your own unless you were a local or you drunkenly fell into a cab that dropped you there because the driver was getting a kickback. I had done my research beforehand and learned it was known as something of a lower-end spot, a little divey, a place where back in 2000, when enforcement was way looser, the girls might do extras if you were a regular and management would look the other way.

Cheetah's didn't have the capacity of the better Vegas clubs like Olympic Gardens or the big names like the Crazy Horse. Its claim to fame was *Showgirls*, the much-maligned Elizabeth Berkley vehicle that was shot there in 1995. Take a look at that scene near the beginning where Nomi asks a table if they'd like a private dance and one guy answers, "Can I suck your tits?" and you'll get the picture.

It was a P&P (panties and pasties) club, which meant that dancers had to keep their G-strings on because the establishment served alcohol. According to the complex laws governing strip clubs in Clark County, booze and nudity couldn't legally go together in public unless you were at the Palomino, which was grandfathered in.

The place looked anything but inviting when we pulled up. The exterior was one unremarkable windowless expanse with stone tiling on the facade. You might have mistaken it for a roadside Italian restaurant if it hadn't been for the ninety-foot sign off to the left proclaiming TOPLESS CLUB. There were bouncers who ushered us in—right past the entrance we paid Diana, who took our cash and photocopied our IDs. I tried not to think too hard about the fact that my presence here was now on someone's record.

Inside, the scene was sadder and danker than I had anticipated. I understood that things were probably different now than they had been fourteen years before, but somehow I had always pictured Ashley in environments that were at least a little bit aspirational; Cheetah's was anything but. There was no artifice here; this place was unabashedly low-rent. The cheap carpeting had some spacelike cosmos pattern in black and purple, and girls in Day-Glo bikinis milled about selling shots. Things were dark, as if we were in some basement bunker. There was a game on the televisions behind the bar.

There was a plastic, lit-from-below stage in the middle of the room, but no one really seemed to be there for the dancing. Crumpled dollar bills were all over, and girls spun lazily around the shiny silver poles; jaded guys clutched dollar bills in their fists and occasionally folded them lengthwise, which seemed to be the signal for a girl to go over to him and squat down for him to stick the bill inside her G-string. The girls onstage weren't making eye contact with anyone, and my primary takeaway was how young and bored they all looked. All the materials and textures were synthetic, whether it was the muted, soft faux velvet upholstery, the neon signs decorating the walls, or the clawlike scrape of fake nails running up a man's arm. No one was particularly sexy or even all that pretty, and as I pictured Ashley among this crowd I couldn't help but consider things in a new way: this was a place she could go to hide. I imagined that the fact that it was so divey was probably part of the appeal to her; she had likely easily gotten a job here as a newbie, and she hadn't had to have the same level of commitment as she would at some of the slicker places. She could try on a different life here part-time, all the while convincing herself it wasn't real.

I knew that in all this speculating I was making a leap. I hadn't been mature enough at the time Ashley told me about her sex work to ask her a lot of questions about how it all felt to her, so I knew I was just project-ing when I assumed that she had to have been performing with a bit of distance. How could it have been any other way? I also knew it was a bit of wishful thinking on my part. Somehow I needed to keep the Ashley I knew—the earlier Ashley—separate from this world in my mind.

At five foot three, with her compact, curvy body and reckless attitude, I could picture Ashley dominating the scene, at least at first, with her body glitter and the Lucite heels and the feeling of superiority I imagined she felt over the customers. She had told me and Nick she was using Prada as a stage name, and I imagined it wasn't because she liked the brand but because it sounded like someone she might like to be: icy, European, with a backstory that took adventurous twists and turns. I knew she liked buy-ing new costumes at clubwear stores, and perhaps she tried on different personas depending on the day. She didn't have a dance background, but I knew she could have picked up how to move in a very watchable way.

As my group settled in to one of the tables and I treated everyone to a round of overpriced prosecco, I realized that Ashley would have been a natural at the business side of things, too: the bait and switch, the push and pull of the authentic versus the image. That she could make the kind of eye contact with a customer that had him imagining their future to-gether or give him a look that made him want to rescue her from it all. She could take the male gaze and monetize it while she could—it was easy to do. She knew just how much to let her real self peek through and when to yank it back. Ashley understood that everyone there was search-ing for something—including her.

I watched the guy next to me be led away to the VIP area, and I had a passing thought that I wondered if Ashley had ever felt, fourteen years ago standing in this same room: in just a short while, I'll be out of here.

Back on the stand, the defense's questioning of Justin has shifted toward Michael: specifically, what they knew about him and when they knew it.

"Do you recall telling police that Ashley thought Mike was a nice guy?" Lindner asks.

"I don't recall."

"Do you know if they slept together?"

Before I can even process that question, Justin answers flatly without seeming taken aback. Clearly he's considered this before. I haven't.

"I heard possibly."

Whoa. I do a double take even though I'm still staring straight ahead. I squeeze my eyes shut and open them again. Yup, still here. No one has moved. My feet are still touching the floor, and my ass is still attached to the seat of this courtroom bench. I did not make up that moment—it really happened. We have just learned that Ashley may have actually had sex with the guy who may later have killed her. This person whom count-less witnesses have now testified to being a creep, a weirdo, someone they didn't want to be around—she was potentially intimate with him, naked with him, vulnerable with him. She honestly didn't see what the others saw or didn't care or—this one's hard for me—was possibly excited by it.

Was he what relationship experts might call a "bad boy"? As in, someone to avoid at all costs if you know what's good for you but of course he's got that irresistible allure? I shiver just thinking about it. Did he have some sort of dangerous sex appeal that worked a number on your pheromone receptors? Would I have thought he was hot if I'd met him in the same circumstances? It's difficult to fathom, especially now, when looking at him only makes me feel dizzy and disgusted.

I would later learn that Gargiulo never seemed to have a problem finding sexual partners. They never do, I can hear Rainn saying. You might have even called him a ladies' man. He had one girlfriend with whom he moved to LA from Illinois; there was another one after that who was a doctor, and in Justin's recollection Gargiulo managed to get a prescription from that one to give to Ashley for her carpal tunnel syndrome—and he'd go on to have two children with different partners before he was arrested in 2008. With that track record, he'd probably be the type to reel in some hot wife while in state prison. I don't think too much about that outrageous side of things, though, as I never encounter anyone from Gargiulo's side in court; the idea of him as an actual partner and father—or even a person in the world—feels safely tucked away in the surreal conceptual realm.

All of this also opens up the complicated notion that things weren't quite as simple as the more appealing interpretation that Ashley's friends were judgmental and catty and she was the inclusive, kinder, more trusting one. That they were like, "This guy's weird, let's blow him off" and she was all, "Stop being such an asshole, he's perfectly fine." Before I heard this sex detail, that was how I wanted to think of her as well. But now. Now? I start to fear that it may have been something different altogether. Maybe her friends were the ones who saw him clearly and she was the one with something reckless, heat seeking, or immature about her. Maybe her risk tolerance had ratcheted way up since getting to LA, and besides, she was twenty-two and invincible and what was the worst that could happen? Did she have a lack of skepticism? Or a lack of scrutiny, a fear instinct, what some might call good judgment? Maybe her time dancing had dulled that part of her, all the transactions with men, security always nearby. Or maybe she never had it to begin with.

I think back to the resigned tone she had when she recounted her night with Oliver. Almost as if it had been easier to sleep with him than not to. Might it have been the same with her murderer?

It feels as if something is breaking open for me. It feels as though I'm starting to make out the outlines of who Ashley was as her own person, not just someone I saw only in reference to me. I was so used to considering us as a pair, and in fact it felt as though our peers and parents regarded us that way, too; when we were younger, it was that Ashley wasn't simply good at piano, she was better at piano than I was; Ashley wasn't just okay at tennis, she was not as good at tennis as I was. When we were older—when we were in New York—Ashley was of course hot on her own, walking down the street with no one around, but put her next to me, and she was "the hot one." You couldn't have two of those, regardless of how I might have looked.

On the flip side, that made me, it seemed, "the smart one" when I was next to Ashley, regardless of how smart she was, because clearly you could be only one or the other—at least that's how the world made it out to be. Of course I guess you could be neither, but it seemed as though put a group or a pair of women or girls together, and someone, somewhere, was ranking you and choosing a winner on those two crucial scales.

I always had a sense that when you were young—when we were both young—somewhere along the way you made the decision, knowingly or not, about which side you'd lead with, looks or brains, perhaps based on a preliminary understanding of which side was already getting more mileage. Things could change in various stages of life, of course, but the stuff that happened to you in puberty and your teen years was what started to force those self-assessments to the surface; later, in young adulthood—first loves, first breakups—they'd gel even further.

What I hadn't understood until recently was that Ashley and I might have developed those self-assessments *in reference to each other*. Next to each other as kids, I was smart and Ashley was perhaps less so; while Ashley was pretty and I was perhaps less so. Over time the descriptions took on weight and became internalized, and soon they felt true on their own whether we were next to each other or not.

I could now imagine Ashley as a twenty-year-old in LA—ground zero for hotness and image-based living and everything in between— taking it all in at first, as if she had found her home. Though as her peer I didn't see it at the time, now I know that of course she had suffered from insecurities, we all did, especially a sensitive person like she was. Of course she was "finding herself," as we all were—as we all still are—and trying to make her way using what she thought were her best—or most easily accessible—assets. Why not make something of the things she had that everyone else couldn't stop validating her for? Why not let them make her money in Vegas and take her on dates with movie stars and who knew what else? You'd have to be crazy not to.

But what if things had gone another way long ago? Maybe with a different best friend, Ashley could have been the smart one. I could have been the hot one—how might our lives have turned out differently? I felt as though, for the first time in this courtroom, I was beginning to get a sense of the possibilities.

Throughout all this, Gargiulo is staring straight ahead, looking intently at the witness on the stand, scrawling furiously on a legal pad, or trying to get his attorney's attention. What must it be like for Chris and Justin and Jen to have to look him in the eye? I'm thankful for being a few rows behind him and mostly just seeing the back of his head. I am, in spite of myself, curious about how the room must look from the witnesses' perspective, as terrifying as it must be. Gargiulo, the creep from almost a decade ago, the creep who sat in their living room and their cars and then maybe mutilated their friend: looking out, challenging, sociopathic, dressed in an orange jumpsuit with a hotshot attorney by his side. Beyond him there's law enforcement and strangers and reporters, and beyond all that, me.

I'm waiting for the elevator on the ninth floor at afternoon break when Lindner rolls up next to me, his ponytailed son by his side. My heart rate picks up; it's that about-to-get-caught-at-something feeling again. I'm wearing a navy blue silk dress and tall stacked heels—I make a point of dressing up for court every day—and for a second I worry that my ankle is going to roll and I'll lose my balance.

I nod at him from the side, but internally I'm hoping we can just keep ignoring each other. It's the elevator way, after all. And furthermore, is this even allowed? Aren't we on opposite sides? Aren't we supposed to be keeping our distance from each other? My eyes stay fixed on the elevator box, willing the numbers to ascend quickly and reach us before anything happens. I can hear his labored breathing and his son adjusting the stack of binders in his hands. Three . . . four . . . there's a long pause on four. The elevator is not moving. Why isn't the elevator moving? What is wrong with this elevator?

"I saw you in our courtroom," Lindner says, his voice coming from my left side. I turn my head to face him, my chest constricting into a twister of adrenaline. He saw me; my delusional cloak of invisibility has fallen off even further. He saw me and wondered about me, just as Christine had, just as Marna Miller had, and likely just as Gargiulo had.

"Yes," I say. "I'm a childhood friend of Ashley's." I don't hold out my hand, and I don't say my name. Part of me is expecting him to go silent after this, like "Oops, OK, wrong answer. Never mind." It's impossible to imagine that he could have anything else to say.

"You're here to bear witness," he says. "It's the right thing to do." He speaks with gravitas, his words carefully chosen and his voice husky. Part of me is impressed. If I had been back at work, I might have called him highly quotable. If only he really were just a character in an article I could hold at arm's length, none of this would be sinking in in the topsy-turvy way that it is. The elevator box is still stuck at four.

I blink. I inhale. I exhale. What's the most enigmatic thing I can think of to respond with? And what's really happening here? Should I hate this person? Should I spit at him? How do this man and his son make sense of defending alleged killers? Are they addicted to the theater of it all? The danger? How can they feel good about trading in slut shaming and a woman's promiscuity as fuel to inflate reasonable doubt? How can they justify this kind of victim blaming? How can they sit next to Gargiulo every day? How can Lindner talk to me right now?

Or is he just a person doing his job? Compartmentalizing his wants and values and natural skepticism and empathy to complete the task at hand? It's a similar logic to the one I use to rationalize when someone is an asshole to me at the DMV. I'm not sure I can make myself buy it in this instance.

"I want to know what happened," I say, giving the line that has become something of a mantra, internally as well as publicly. It is becoming truer and truer by the day, yet with each person I deliver it to, the meaning shifts slightly. Even still, it is one of the few things I know with confidence.

"Sometimes that can turn out to be a lot to handle, knowing what happened," Lindner says. There he goes with those aphorisms again. So quizzical, so dense. So inscrutable. We stare straight ahead again, settling into the natural pause of the exchange: he spoke; I spoke; he spoke; I spoke; he spoke again—a perfect conversational pentagon. There is nothing left to say. Is there anything left to say?

As if on cue, the elevator doors open.

13

SOME GRAPHIC IMAGES

IF THERE WERE an award for the witness in this hearing who would be most likely to play himself in the movie version of this story, it would go to Mark Durbin. Ashley's next-door neighbor, sometime lover, and the property manager of her house is so camera-ready, it's almost as if he'd been created by screenwriters, right down to the way he rubs his brow when he's nervous and the way his ass looks in those black jeans as he takes the stand.

Even his name is movie star–sounding, and in fact, he has a long list of IMDB credits, as I learn after googling him about thirty seconds after he starts speaking. His bio reveals that he really is one of those quintessential Hollywood types: the slash person. Waiter-slash-actor, makeup-artist-slash-model—you know the type; they have them in New York, too. Unless you're a casting director or an agent meeting them at an audition, you can always recognize them by the fact that they're way too good-looking for whatever situation you've found them in. They are the most magnetic people at the club door, fixing your shower, refilling your water glass. Sometimes they don't realize this; most of the time they do. For Durbin, I discover, the slash-actor part hasn't changed much in the past decade or so, but the whatever part has been filled in with everything from handyman to tour guide to dockworker. Dockworker?

Gossip outside the courtroom—from Christine, from the Internet— is that Durbin is now married to the woman he was with when he and Ashley were hooking up. She's a dancer, and they have kids now, and this whole thing is terribly uncomfortable for him. She ostensibly forgave him somehow, somewhere, at some point back then, but now with this hearing he's forced to humiliate himself—and her and his family—all over again, re-embodying the guy he once was: a handyman who was cheating on his partner with the sexy girl next door. If only he were allowed to truly leave all that behind—to get away with it, as it were. Poor, poor, hot handyman. Ashley never got that choice, though, so to me at least a little squirming in his seat seems as though it should be more than tolerable, given what happened to her.

He's also disturbed by the presence of press, I am told. He's already aware that he doesn't come off well, and now he has to deal with potentially having it affect his slash career, dredging up this "association" he had put behind him. He's weighing the competing impulses of telling the truth versus controlling his image; you can tell by his reticence to answer even the most basic things. Which will win out?

I can't take my eyes off of him, even as he's getting testy under questioning. He looks to be about six foot two, he's tall and broad-shouldered and muscled, and for the first time I get a glimpse into a part of Ashley's life that really does look appealing. I can clearly imagine the effect this guy must have had on her back in 2001, because he's having it on me right now.

"A lot of these questions, it's like the first page of Homer's *Iliad*.

I mean there is so much," Durbin says, an oddly contrived response to the question of whether or not the figure he reported seeing in front of Ashley's house later that night after he left her could have been Ashton Kutcher.

"There are no wine-dark seas in this case," says Lindner. Eye roll. Defense attorneys, I have noticed, find it hard to resist opportunities for a bit of showboating.

"Let's move on," says the judge.

Durbin is in a difficult position, though, and it's clear that Lindner is setting him up to look suspicious to drum up more reasonable doubt that Gargiulo is definitely the killer. This guy was right there: they were involved, he was cheating. The potential motive—although not the most persuasive one—is right there.

I don't for a second believe it could be him, though, from the simple manner of Ashley's death itself, let alone that I just don't buy it on a gut level. Ashley was stabbed forty-seven times, brutally and with extreme force. Durbin is clearly strong enough to have overpowered Ashley, sure, but the average stabbing murder victim suffers far fewer wounds—look up a typical murder case, and you're much more likely to find stab wound numbers topping out around fifteen, per my research. In other words— at least following my layperson's logic—whoever did this had to have been a professional killer, a professional psychopath, and probably both.

I am impressed that Lindner is leading things so well, bringing up disputes Durbin had with past female employers and at least one temporary restraining order filed against him. The very tight timeline of the night's events is striking, as well: somewhere between around 7 p.m. and sex with Durbin and the time that Ashton Kutcher arrived, around 10 p.m., Ashley was killed.

"Sir, if you were one of the last persons to see Ashley Ellerin alive, were you the first person to see her dead?" shouts Lindner.

"I'm going to object," says Miller.

"I never saw her dead," sighs Durbin.

". . . Overruled."

Things are getting a little scary as the defense closes in. What are they getting at? Why is Durbin coming apart so quickly? It doesn't take much work to erode any sympathy this guy might have started with. Maybe he's just too good-looking? Or maybe it's just me; I can't stand cheaters.

I feel a tiny pang for the panic he must be experiencing, but at least in this instance, I'm glad it's not Ashley's active sex life Lindner's harping on as a means to convey that we can't be sure his client is the killer. The scrutiny is at present focused on just one man and just one sex act.

In a series of cross-examinations and redirects, both Miller and Lindner probe Durbin in excruciating detail to recount the chain of foreplay that resulted in him and Ashley having sex that night. It's cringeworthy and more than a little bit exciting to hear—a prurient look into Ashley's private means of seduction, her tools, her gestures, her bag of tricks.

It all started with a faulty ceiling fan or light and then proceeded like a porno fantasy come to life.

"I wasn't so sure the light thing was really an issue or it was a reason to get me over to visit," Durbin explains, by way of giving context to the fact that he was in Ashley's apartment only hours before her murder. She had called him to come fix her ceiling light, and he was hesitant to go over. He guessed she was probably after more than just his handyman capabilities. How typical, and cheap, to call the dead woman the instigator. I knew I'd never seen Ashley initiate any approach to a man—why would she, given all the attention she got?

The two of them had already hooked up a few times, but Durbin was trying to play it straight, as he lived next door in the same building as his longtime girlfriend and he already felt bad about how far he had let it go with Ashley in the past.

Later, Chris would tell me that he and Justin did not approve. "You're better than just a side ho," Justin would tease her. And Chris thought Durbin was a bit of a sleazeball. But none of that mattered to Ashley. Just as always, she would do what she wanted, when she wanted.

"We had been intimate prior to that, but never really completely consummated anything," Durbin says.

Does that mean oral?

A few years later, Chris would tell me that he had always been sketched out by Durbin. Chris said he would just about bet his car that he and Ashley had done it before that night.

Once Durbin fixed the light, he says, they "hung out for probably about an hour." I've imagined time and again what that might have meant. Did it mean kissing? Did they lounge on the couch and talk about politics? What did Ashley do to move things along? I could only imagine I'd have been sitting there nervously. An older guy, attractive, a guy who had all the power—how could this have ever been my show to run? I would have waited, waited, waited for something to happen, never considering for a moment that I could have set things in motion myself.

Durbin's testimony, in all its detail, continued. Ashley said she needed to take a shower as she was going out later. She invited Durbin into the bathroom, and they kept talking from opposite sides of the shower curtain as Ashley rinsed off. I thought about that move for a second. It seemed coy and brazen at once. Showering while a guest is over, inviting him into your space so he can stand on the other side of a flimsy piece of plastic while hot water pours down on you and steam rises around your body. Of course he's picturing you naked behind the curtain, you've made it easy for him—you've drawn the picture for him almost completely; maybe he can even see your silhouette in shadow. Of course you might not have been surprised if suddenly he appeared naked behind you as you stood facing the shower head, soaping up your hair with Pantene. "Oh, hello," you'd say as you slowly turned around and brought your lips to his. Everything has fallen into place according to your plan.

But Durbin didn't move things that way, at least that time, at least so he says. When Ashley was ready to get out, she asked him to step out of the bathroom. Then it was on to the bedroom. What happened next was mercifully glossed over, but here's how I imagine it: Ashley's hair is wet, her skin glistens with water, as well. She holds a towel wrapped around herself with one hand; Durbin follows her into her room. There's a candle already lit, and the room is otherwise dark. She turns, facing him, and slowly drops the towel. She is confident and naive at once, and it is impossible to take your eyes off her.

I think of the way she strolled up and down the hallway of my one-bedroom apartment more than a decade ago, naked but for a black thong. She seemed barely aware of her nakedness, how she appeared, and how it might be taken by whoever else was in the room, but part of her also seemed to know she looked fantastic. It was a lack of self-consciousness bred from experience: she had a body that she knew paid the bills, that made men make stupid decisions. Walking around naked in front of her childhood friend was harmless, but I wondered if self-doubt ever did creep in.

"When you did have intercourse with Ashley, were either of you loud with your emotions? Either of you scream during this passionate . . . encounter?" asks Deputy District Attorney Miller. Yeesh. Poor Durbin, I think in my head for the first time. How incredibly awkward and invasive to have to recount something like this in public. What could Miller be getting at?

"I wouldn't say silent, but it was more intimate," Durbin says. "It wasn't like anything anybody was going to hear—part of my concern was that the parking lot was right outside the bedroom window." The parking lot next door being the one his girlfriend would soon be driving into. Classy. "I left hurriedly to some degree and reluctantly to another," he says. "I recall her telling me that . . . she had fallen for me."

He sighs. "She said she didn't want me to have to leave," he says, and that she didn't want to go out anymore either. The room is silent. I look at my knees. Here's the moment when the acknowledgment of loss descends. When voices start to talk more softly, slowly, it's when the victim becomes human once again, and by human, I mean we remember that she's dead. We're backing up against the crime and turning over the contours of what might have gone differently had this person stayed just a little longer, left a little earlier, taken a different turn that day. We see guilt writ large and painful personal reckoning. It's happened with each witness: for Chris it was the moment when he and Ashley first met Gargiulo on the street; for Justin it was Gargiulo's hand on his in the car; and for Durbin, it's knowing that he could have stayed longer that night—she wanted him to stay! What if he had stayed?

It's also the first time any of the testimony has revealed something of Ashley's vulnerability. Maybe she did really want this guy: even with her celebrity hookups, her big-ticket escort gigs, and her life-of-the-party sex appeal, she couldn't always get what she wanted. Here came the limits of her sexual power; it could get her into a man's arms for a night or two, sure, but it couldn't necessarily get her into his heart. She had worked herself into a situation that was clearly ill advised: falling for someone who was taken. No matter how hot you were, that kind of mess always ended in tears.

But maybe Durbin really did have feelings for Ashley—girlfriend aside. I had heard from a family friend that for six months after her death, he had called the Ellerins regularly to see if there was any new information.

"I'm the kind of person, as a man, that, yes I care about the security of women that I'm involved with and women in general, whether it was my sister or my mom or my girlfriend," Durbin says defensively when he's asked about the circumstances under which he left Ashley's house after they had just had sex. He called her when he got home but he thinks he probably got her answering machine. He can't remember. He also said he sent some wistful longing looks toward her house, but mostly after the sex stuff his testimony that day ends with a whimper. The last known person to see Ashley alive has finished his story. If only he had more to say—if only there were more to say. The only person who would be able to say more is her killer.

Unexpectedly, Durbin's words are some of the hardest for me to listen to. What is it about this guy and his swagger and his fleeting sexual encounter with Ashley that is somehow sticking with me? Something about the testimony felt particularly unjust. This whole thing is outrageously unjust, obviously, but Durbin seems like a living embodiment of just how unjust. Why did this guy get to be married—to a woman he cheated on!—and have a family and act as though we should feel sorry for him because he has to dredge up the past by (gasp) talking about his transgressions, whereas Ashley is murdered, robbed of what could have been seventy-five more years of life, and she wasn't even cheating? I have lived long enough to know better than to expect life to be fair, but occasionally a somewhat Draconian idea of crime and punishment flares up in me around the subject of infidelity. None of my previous boyfriends cheated on me—to the best of my knowledge—but I have always reserved a particularly bitter judgment toward people who cheated and "got away with it." Maybe I am also just fried on courtroom dramas. My mind is flitting about on this and other subjects, but mostly I'm just itching to leave Department 108 for the day. It has been a long one, and I'm looking forward to a glass of wine and maybe a burger. Maybe something with avocado. Or bacon.

Yeah, bacon. I'm gathering my things and standing up to leave the room when I see DA Miller coming toward me.

"Do you have a moment?" she asks. I look behind me for a second. Is she really talking to me? Christine and most everyone else have left at this point. The bailiffs and the other lawyers are collecting their binders and straightening the place up. I nod. She motions for me to come up through the gate over to where her table and chairs are.

"How's everything been so far?" she asks, warmly and with care in her voice, almost like a librarian or grade school teacher.

"Oh, you know. Fine," I say, instantly realizing that nothing was, but still, that's what you say. Same old same old. What was I supposed to say? What is she asking of me? Where is this going? Did I do something wrong? This feels like the sort of special attention that I'm not sure I need right now.

"I just want to let you know that tomorrow we're going to be showing some graphic images of the crime scene," she begins. "I always try to warn friends and family members beforehand so they can leave the room at that time. This is not how you want to remember your friend. It's better to keep her in your mind as you knew her."

What is the Ashley I have in my mind? It's hard to choose just one image. Is it us as girls? Young and soft-featured in Esprit stirrup pants and scrunchies? Or is it Ashley the last time I saw her—plucked and manicured and tanned in seven-inch Lucite heels? Maybe I do want to see this final Ashley, to bear witness, and to catalogue it with all the rest. Miller's tone has a directive, officious, almost threatening quality to it, like if I "disobey" there will be consequences.

I understand the simple present tense she has just used to assert her authority and her experience—"I always try to warn friends and family members"—and I know that the force in her voice is only trying to protect me from what she is sure will make things worse for me. I appreciate this, even as I receive the information as if I am watching myself receive the information.

I look down at my blue silk dress, my Marni heels, the same ones I nearly fell off of when Lindner approached me at the elevator. I am wearing one of the new outfits I had bought myself when I first started at *New York*, still dressing up for my new job and hoping to pass as an adult. Somewhere along the way I realized I had become one. In the courtroom I had seen in a new way what it looks like when a life is cut off at twenty-two. All the messy baby fat of emotional immaturity still stuck on you for eternity, paraded out for everyone to see.

I'm lucky that isn't me anymore, even though my immaturity back then expressed itself very differently than Ashley's had. I've become a grown woman in all the ways she never got to, among them: I can enjoy attention from men and not define my life around it. I can sit with myself and feel my feelings. I can admit vulnerability and communicate to others when I need help. For that and much more, I feel grateful for the almost ten more years I have on her.

I know immediately that I won't agree to do as Miller is telling me to do, or at least I will need some time to think about it. I won't do as she says just because she is telling me to, just because it's the recommended behavior for friends and family of the victim. I will need a much better reason than that.

I wish I hadn't been given this warning.

"If I remember, I'll take a short pause and look at you before I get to the graphic photos, and that's when you should leave the room," she goes on. "In case I'm too busy to do that, I'm just going to show you a few of the photos now and you'll know when you should leave. Don't worry, I'm not going to show you the bad ones."

The bad ones, eh? Like the ones full of blood and pain and violence like I've never encountered in real life? The ones I've already pictured in my mind countless times? The ones I am terrified of yet masochistically drawn to, now that I know they exist? Those ones?

Miller opens a black plastic three-ring binder on the table, each loose-leaf page laminated in a plastic sleeve, reminding me of the way that Ashley and I would make our manuals for the Young Inventor's contests we entered together in elementary school. Miller's binder looks almost exactly like our old binders. My mind jumps to the weird fact that capital murder trials and grade school projects use the same supplies, and then Miller starts to describe what we're seeing.

"Here's the outside of her house," she's saying. And there's Ashley's yellow house indeed, the one on Pinehurst I had looked at on Google Street View more than a hundred times, only in this image the place is crisscrossed with yellow crime scene tape bisecting the view. My heart is pounding, even more than the other day with Lindner at the elevator. Miller flips the page, and we see a hallway. "This is her hallway," she says. There's beige carpeting—the nylon kind with the flat loop weave—narrow walls, and more of that police tape. What's at the end of the hallway? Is Ashley back there? Can she hear us?

"This is when you should leave the room," Miller says. "Like I said, I'll try to remember to pause and make eye contact with you when we get here, but if I don't, just remember that when you see this picture, you should leave." I nod, but half of me wants to cry out: Go on! Show me the rest! Take me to her. Now. Please. I can handle it. I must handle it. I've never been more prepared for anything in my life than I am for this. This is what I came here for, isn't it? Without knowing when it will happen, part of me understands that just then I butted right up against the thing that could potentially break this wide open for me in my head: a through line, a final punctuation mark, the *Finis* in *Finis origine pendet*.

Instead I say nothing. I am afraid of not appearing as I should, hewing to the expectations she has of me, a friend of the victim, a victim myself. I am afraid of looking demented, of sullying her trust in me and her belief that I am a good-hearted person who showed up in this place to honor her long-lost friend. I should be taking care of my treasured memories, holding them tight in a locked vault in my mind. I should be protecting them from anyone or anything that could encroach upon them.

I know in that moment that tomorrow I will stay in the room.

"Thank you," I mumble weakly. And then we make a bit of small talk about parking and traffic and some such typical meaningless LA filler, and suddenly I am back in my rental car in the underground parking structure not quite remembering the steps I took to get there. It is hot, and I reach for a half-drunk bottle of water I tossed on the floor in the morning and take a sip. The liquid is the temperature of soup that's been sitting out.

After a few more minutes I put the key in the ignition, and it's only then that I notice that my hands are shaking.

That night I dream of her, for the first time in a long time.

We were at the trial—her trial—both of us somehow. She was my age, and we were watching everything together. Lindner was there, the mood was light.

"What did you do on the break?" I could hear Lindner say to Gargiulo in the front. We're waiting for the proceedings to start, and the judge hasn't entered yet. "Let me guess—you read feminist polemics," he added, and then they both guffawed.

Ashley was wearing elegant teal leather low heels with pointy-toes—they could have been Manolos. She had on a tailored gray suit with a smart single-breasted blazer and a pencil skirt. Her hair was her natural brown, cut short in a bob. She looked businesslike with a fashion edge, like a lawyer but "Julianna Margulies from the *The Good Wife*"–style.

She sat in the front, and I was a few rows back. I went to her. We had not seen each other in many, many years. "What are you doing here?" she asked, laughing, happy. Isn't all of this hilarious? Isn't it surreal and just the funniest thing you could ever imagine? It's as if the both of us have inhaled nitrous oxide. I burst into tears, crying, crying, crying hard, like the time I had surgery on my wrist and the anesthesia wouldn't leave my body for a whole day. "I've always been here," I said, my nose running all over the place. "It was you who wasn't here."

I wake up with a start—a jolt, an electric stab in the middle of my ribs. I am on an air mattress in a dark room in West Hollywood. Marisa and Rainn's cat has slipped through the door and is perched on Rainn's desk in front of me, her eyes glowing an uncaring topaz. My apartment is empty in Brooklyn. My parents are asleep in New Jersey. I am scared. I am safe. I am scared. I am safe.

My flight back to New York is at nine in the evening. I have packed my bags and am set to drive my rental car directly to LAX after court. I am tired. The rest of my sleep was fitful after waking up in the middle of the night, and the morning time-change bounce I typically get in my first few days of flying west has faded. Tomorrow will be New York, the subway, my office. Tomorrow all of this will be behind me.

When I reach my regular spot in Department 108—last row to the left—I stretch my legs out like a courtroom veteran. I feel calm knowing I am on my way home. Christine is already here, same with the woman from *Dateline* and another from CBS. Lindner and his son make their way in, and behind them is Miller. She nods at me as she walks up to the front, stacks of folders in her hand.

I am a known entity in this courtroom now, and that fact is not lost on me as I prepare for the pictures. Today I am the only one in this room besides the defendant who knew Ashley, and almost everyone in this room knows this. I know that people will be looking at me when the photos come up, that my reaction will be observed. So will his. That it will amplify the pressure, that people will be able to see my feelings. DA Miller will see me as well, and she won't understand why I am still sitting there watching. I'm not sure I will, either.

I have no frame of reference for what might happen to my body when I see them, but I am trying to prepare for multiple scenarios. Noises might come out of me, I have considered. Noises I have never produced before and rarely heard. They might be loud, they might be alarming to others. For this I am sorry in advance. Shooting pains in my head might overtake me, a spontaneous onset of deep unrest within my skull. I might also begin to feel light-headed and slump down in my seat. Maybe I won't be able to take all of this in even if I think I want to. Vomiting is another reaction I am wondering about, but it seems the least likely.

I have decided that at the moment the pictures start—the house, then the hallway—I'm going to look at the ground. If DA Miller is motioning for me to leave the room at that point, I won't be able to see her. She will have to continue, and then I will raise my head. No one else will know that I was warned about that moment; the only person who will be confused is Miller, but I'm sure it will be minor. She has much bigger things to contend with.

When the judge arrives, he announces that we will be adjourning before lunch today and that testimony will be out of order because of a certain forensic investigator's vacation schedule. Instead of starting with the pictures, we will be starting with testimony relating to 2005 murder victim Maria Bruno. My anxiety starts to pick up. I have no idea how much evidence is about to be discussed regarding Bruno, but I do know we now have only four hours in the day in which to get through it so we can resume the original timeline and Miller can present the crime scene photos. Part of me feels cold thinking in those terms. This other victim—a thirty-four-year-old, stunningly beautiful mother of four from El Salvador who lived in the LA suburb El Monte—deserves as much time and attention as Ashley does for the facts of her story to be told. Only her friends aren't here, no one is, and I have spent the past twelve hours in knots preparing for something else to happen. I haven't bargained for Maria.

Over the past few days, during testimony and later in my research, I have picked up bits and pieces about Maria and gotten a little more background on the other charges against Gargiulo and the gruesome crime he was ultimately arrested for. Christine also emailed me when I got back to New York with snapshots from the testimony I had missed. From the lengthy story she published about the case a few months later in *LA Weekly*, I learned that in late 2003, Gargiulo had begun a relationship with Grace Kwak, a woman he had met on Match.com and with whom he would later have a child. By 2005, they were living together in an apartment complex in El Monte. Kwak moved out during Thanksgiving weekend, saying that the relationship had become abusive. Maria Bruno moved into the building around the same time, and just ten days later, she was founded murdered at home, her body mutilated. Police ran the records of neighbors in the building, but no one had a background of major criminal activity.

I learned that by 2008, Gargiulo was married and living in Santa Monica, across an alley from a woman named Michelle Murphy, who often worked out in the space between the buildings. On April 28, 2008, he allegedly climbed through the window of Murphy's bedroom and began stabbing her as she slept. It was dark, and he covered his head with the hood of his sweatshirt and used his dominant left hand to wield the knife while he held her down with his right. Fortunately for her, she had been sleeping naked, and the wounds oozing blood against her bare skin made her slippery as she raged and roiled fighting him. He had trouble restraining her, and he accidentally caught his hand on the blade as he hammered down blows upon her. Then, panicking, he tried to switch the knife into his other hand. In that moment, she was able to kick him off her. He murmured a slurred "I'm sorry" and then darted back out the window.

The victim was unable to ID him, but she didn't need to—detectives found a trail of his blood leading straight from her building to Gargiulo's. He was arrested in June and charged with Murphy's attempted murder, and later that year charges for Maria Bruno's and Ashley's murders with burglary were added. He was also a person of interest in the unsolved murder of his high school classmate Tricia Pacaccio in Glenview, Illinois, in 1993, but that wasn't being handled by California authorities.

I take a deep breath. I slip out for a bathroom break, and I take an extra long time washing my hands. When I return to the room, the same witness is on the stand, discussing what to me sounds like exactly the same thing as he was before I left the room. It's all very technical. I've stopped taking as many notes. More expert witnesses are testifying about intricate measurements of blood spatters and footprints around this other crime scene. There are diagrams and references to angles and circumferences. They are mostly in black and white.

I find myself reading the news on my laptop, occasionally G-chatting with a friend from New York who's bored at his office. Time ticks by slowly, and then all at once we are into the last hour before lunch. It is nearing break time, and part of me is holding out hope that this witness will abruptly end her testimony and then we'll get to the photos under the wire, and part of me is making peace with the fact that I won't be seeing them, at least not today. I am slowly letting go of the personal reckoning I did to be ready for this moment: my plan of obfuscation toward Miller, the smooth rock I had put into my bag to hold on to in case I felt faint. I would release those things into the "unlived experiences" file. Perhaps I would use them another time; perhaps I wouldn't.

The judge calls a recess until the following morning. I knew it would be coming, but I still feel a jolt of panic. Suddenly I don't want to accept things going down this way. I was ready to make my own decision, and now it's being made for me. It doesn't feel fair. Should I change my flight? Should I tell work something came up? Should I stay here for as long as this takes? How long will that be? How much would that cost? Would a real friend change her flight to be there? Would Ashley want me to?

I had already told the DA I was leaving today, so if I did show up here again tomorrow, it might look even weirder. Either way, I have a little bit more time to decide. I go up to the front of the room anyway and say good-bye to Miller. "I'm leaving today," I say. "I guess the pictures aren't happening." Part of me is hoping that she can read my mind and she'll offer to show them to me right then. She doesn't. She is kind, she speaks in platitudes—"It's for the best"—and we shake hands.

On the elevator ride down to the exit I'm still feeling up in the air. Am I leaving tonight, or am I staying? Do I take this as a sign that I'm not meant to see these pictures, or do I take it as a sign that I'm supposed to dig in harder? Which is right, and which is correct? Who can help me decipher what my heart knows to be true? Would Rainn know the answer?

I'm making my way out the door to the sidewalk when I see Lindner and his son smoking cigarettes at the top of the ramp. I will have to do an about-face to avoid them. Of course I wouldn't be able to just slip out of the state in peace. I nod and they nod. I am exhausted and emotionally depleted. It feels like as good a time as any to try out my new skills: I am now a person who can casually chat with high-powered attorneys who are defending my childhood best friend's killer in a capital murder case. Sure, why not?

We talk about my travel plans; they ask about my job. I have gotten over the idea that we aren't allowed to be talking at all, and now I just wonder what we are allowed to be talking about. I yearn to ask them something about the case, about Gargiulo, about what he's really like. What he says to them and how he makes sense of this and why they're doing it all. Instead I say nothing.

"He's evil," the son says at one point. Whoa. Okay. The two then go on to explain a bit more about their process, how their job in a capital trial is to make sure their client receives the protections he's entitled to under the law. I take this as permission to discuss the case, and I tell them I thought I'd see the pictures today. "You don't want to see that," says the son. "She was mutilated. Her head was practically severed." Will I be back for the trial? they ask. Will I speak?

I respond with something, but I'm not really listening to myself as I talk. Did I say yes? Did I say maybe? I look out into the parking lot ahead of me: the big space, probably more than an acre, reserved for jurors and legal officers of the court. The cars are white and red and blue and silver and black. Behind me I can hear someone stopping to chat with Lindner; the tone is jovial. They haven't seen each other in a while, it's a good-old-boy "You still kicking around?" kind of conversation. In two years this lot will be covered in green, the cars moved out and the ticket booth knocked down and the whole thing filled in with palm trees and open lawn and pink benches where homeless people and city workers will eye each other warily. In three years after that, I'll be back here getting prepped to testify in Ashley's trial.

I don't know any of that yet, though. I don't know what will happen next or all the times I'll roll this moment over and over in my head. What I do know—what I feel suddenly as if a drug has just kicked in—is that it's time to go home.

PART
FOUR

14

GLENVIEW

IN THE MONTHS after the preliminary hearing, my mind was a jumble of names and dates and facts and allegiances, like the climactic scene in a hacker movie where the computer screen finally floods with blinking characters after a big data dump and the nerds' eyes go googly. You intuit that whatever's turned up is valuable and hard-won, but what does it all mean? How do you organize it all and make use of it?

Who was good, who was bad, and what those days in Department 108 meant to me took a similar amount of unpacking. The answers were less clear-cut than I would have expected going into things. Everything didn't just neatly distill down into narratives like "Defense = evil; prosecution = valiant" or some similar binary. After all, I had talked to Lindner, I had heard empathy in his voice, even though the next day he had turned around and questioned witnesses about Ashley's pole dancing and how much of a party girl she was. Which was an act? Or maybe both were? I had talked to the prosecutor and felt comforted by how kind she had been to me, but maybe some of that was serving her own interests as well. Also: Do they all genuinely believe in the death penalty? An eye for an eye—really? It would require years of mental inventory taking to sort through it all; there were too many threads and obscured motivations doubling back on top of themselves.

The trial was still ahead of me and with it a chance to review and sort through the information anew and hear a verdict delivered. This, it would say, is what happened. I knew that of course that would never be the final word on my feelings about Ashley's death—those feelings would grow and change just as I would over the years—but part of me still fantasized about the potential for finality that a verdict might bring. I had been told that, on average, trials usually started about twelve to eighteen months following the preliminary hearing, so that put things at mid- to late 2011.

Meanwhile, jarring images from that week would come back at random moments and stop me in my tracks like PTSD-induced flashbacks. A walk up West Broadway near my office where Ashley and I had gone into that clubwear store all those years before would trigger a flash of that party photo they'd kept showing in court—the smiling faces with Ashley in the middle and that mock turtleneck and the white flower in her hair. Youth, beauty—not a fear in sight on any of them. It made me want to hop a train to New Jersey and hug my parents, to feel protected and safe from the unknown, if even for just a moment.

I called my building super to fix a leak under my kitchen sink, and I'd see Durbin's face at the other end of the line and hear his words about Ashley and the light fixture. "I wasn't so sure the light thing was really an issue or it was a reason to get me over to visit," he'd drawled. That jaw-line, those perfectly weathered black jeans—the swagger of entitlement I projected onto him. For a second I'd commit to never letting myself be vulnerable to another man again, and I wouldn't notice until a moment later that I was shaking my head in the air. I'd blink my eyes at the too-bright sun overhead in New York and suddenly be in California, outside with Lindner and his son on that last day at Clara Shortridge Foltz, emotional exhaustion and anxiety dropping down on me all over again. How quickly I passed out on that flight home, the crease on my cheek I woke up with after leaning against the plane cabin wall. How my clothes still smelled like court when I unpacked. Was any of it really in the past? Would it ever be?

Part of me also felt as though crucial pieces in my understanding were still missing. While I continued to try to make sense of what had lead Ashley to end up dead in her home in Hollywood and me to a courtroom in Los Angeles to bear witness to it all, there was a third and very large piece of the puzzle that remained a mystery: her alleged killer.

Who was this guy, and why had his path really crossed with Ashley's—and later mine? Michael Gargiulo had been charged with Ashley's murder, Maria Bruno's, and the attempted murder of Michelle Murphy, with DNA linking him to the last two, plus he was still a person of interest in the Illinois murder of his high school classmate, Tricia Pacaccio, in 1993. As I'd learned from the hearing, he wasn't a hit man or a wild drug addict or another type you instinctively knew to avoid. He had been "passing" for years, and he had infiltrated himself into Ashley's life and social group without too much difficulty before allegedly killing her when he was just twenty-five years old.

All of us have an origin story, some place where we started from or some inciting incident that makes us who we were. So much would always be unknowable, I understood, but I wondered if perhaps learning more about Gargiulo's past could help fill in some holes. Since I hadn't known Gargiulo in the "outside world," as Jen, Chris, and Justin had, I couldn't attest to his creepiness or experience any unprejudiced gut feeling about him, since I had only ever encountered him handcuffed and charged with murder. I wanted to come to some conclusion on my own, if that was possible, about if he had done it.

If I were a spiritual sort, I might have called what happened next divine timing, but suffice it to say I was excited and a little spooked that just a little while later I received an email from a producer named Doug Longhini at CBS's *48 Hours* who was working on a show about the Illinois case against Gargiulo. He had attended the preliminary hearing in LA after I'd left and had gotten my information from another CBS producer I had met there, and he was interested in talking to me about Ashley for background. (Before I left court, I'd exchanged emails with Christine from *LA Weekly* and the two other media people I had met in hopes of keeping in touch about the things I'd be missing later in the week.)

In his email, Doug explained that he had been following the Gargiulo case for the past two years, focusing on Gargiulo's connection to the Tricia Pacaccio murder from 1993. He went on to say that even though Gargiulo's DNA had been found on Tricia's fingernails, the Cook County state's attorney had refused to bring charges against him.

Doug had interviewed Tricia's family the month before, and though they were still deeply traumatized, they had participated in the interview because they hoped the CBS show could convince Illinois authorities to take another look at the case, especially given all the new information that was coming out in the hearings in California.

I was intrigued, not just because I was eager to learn more about Gargiulo and what had happened to Tricia but also because I was curious about how a real investigative crime reporter/producer behaved and what it looked like not to have a personal stake in things. Doug had approached victims and their families with the conviction that the work he was doing could help bring them justice and, perhaps, peace. I envied that moral clarity and sense of purpose. I didn't feel that my own personal auditing and researching and observing was contributing to anything as lofty as justice or peace for a grieving family, but still it felt important in its own way.

We met for a coffee at a place near my office. Doug was kind-looking, my father's age, and I came away impressed with his sensitivity and experience. I spoke about Ashley and the questions I had about her last year of life, but mostly I found myself listening a lot more than talking. The mandate of his show was always justice for victims and their families, he said. Justice for Ashley, I thought. What would that look like?

In addition to loads of biographical details about Gargiulo that I hadn't learned at the hearing, Doug shared a guiding principle about his reporting practice that I continue to think about to this day: "We're not in the business of trying to convince someone why they should talk to us. They have to have their own reason."

With that in mind, he told me, his production would not be approaching 2008 victim Michelle Murphy. The experience of having to talk about the before and after again would be too disturbing. It just wasn't worth it. Doug told me he had had some email and telephone contact with Ashley's father but that it had been inconsistent. Just when it seemed that they would be close to making a plan to meet, something would come up for Mr. Ellerin.

Part of me felt reassured hearing that Doug had also experienced difficulty reaching the Ellerins. I had often wondered if I should be trying harder to connect with them, beyond the multiple unanswered letters I had sent over the years. Should I send them something? Should I show up at their home in California? All of that felt terribly invasive. I realized that subconsciously I had all along been hoping that they would have their own reason for wanting to talk to me. By this point, I had come to accept that they did not.

• • •

I would remember Doug's words again two years later when I met Chris outside court for the first time, watching his raw emotions give way to delicate insights. Someone might not tell you his motivation straight out for sharing their story, I saw—they might not understand it themselves— but if you listened closely and gave them time, things would begin to make sense for both of you.

Doug painted Gargiulo to be a cocky bully. He told me how he had driven a dark green pickup truck and had done stints as an HVAC guy and a bouncer in LA but would tell anyone who'd listen that he'd been *thisclose* to becoming an Olympic boxer. For a time he had thought about trying to make it as an actor—his first year out in LA, a USC film student had cast him as a boxer in his graduate thesis, a short feature called "Boxing's Been Good to Me."

I found the movie on YouTube as soon as I got back to the office: Gargiulo appears in the film only briefly, meeting the protagonist in the ring for a practice bout and leveling him in less than thirty seconds with a nasty right hook. In the background at the end of the scene, you can see him raising his fists above his head in a victory dance. The main character is slumped over on the floor and later told by his disappointed coach, "You just ain't got what it takes. You gotta be a killer inside."

As the credits rolled, I felt dirty. The short was dated 2000, so depending on the time of year, it might have been filmed only a matter of months before Gargiulo allegedly killed Ashley. Tricia Pacaccio was already seven years dead. This was the first time I had seen him younger and in his prime, close to the way Ashley would have seen him, not the drawn character with the shaved head and orange jumpsuit I had seen in court. The difference was striking.

Twenty-four-year-old Gargiulo was tall and muscular, his upper body covered in menacing tattoos: a rabid-looking dog on his left forearm, a skull on his right shoulder, the Chinese character for "champion" across his back. I wanted to think that I could pick out the violence inside him already, just from that momentary glimpse on-screen, but in truth, all I saw was awkward acting.

Five months later, I stood in front of Gargiulo's childhood home in Glenview, Illinois. I had driven there on a few hours' break from a wedding weekend in Chicago. It was the quintessential upper-middle-class suburban town, straight out of a John Hughes movie. I hadn't planned on going to the house when I'd booked the tickets earlier in the summer, but then I got to my hotel and I realized I'd never be closer to where Ashley's alleged killer—an alleged serial killer—had grown up. By itself, it might not have been a place I would have sought out on my own, but since I was already most of the way there, it felt too big to ignore. Maybe if I saw it—maybe if I saw where Tricia had died, too—I'd feel a sense of connection. It was like those "Dearly Departed" tours of Hollywood, where they take you on a bus around to all the sites where celebrities met their end and tourists can take pictures. For a time, I'd heard, they had been going past Ashley's house, Ashton Kutcher and all.

None of the Gargiulos lived there anymore—Michael's siblings had scattered in different directions in the years after Tricia had died, and then his father moved across town. The house was just around the corner from a primary school, with a banner out front reading CHARACTER COUNTS IN GLENVIEW. It looked a bit desolate now; there was a motorcycle with a FOR SALE sign leaning against the big tree in the front yard.

"I knew this moment well," Geoff Dyer wrote in *Out of Sheer Rage* after arriving at the nondescript house in Sicily where D. H. Lawrence briefly lived. "You look and look and try to summon up feelings which don't exist. You try saying a mantra to yourself, 'D. H. Lawrence lived here.' You say, 'I am standing in the place he stood, seeing the things he saw . . .' but nothing changes, everything remains exactly the same: a road, a house with sky above it and the sea glinting in the distance."

This is where a murderer grew up, this is where a murderer grew up, I repeated to myself, just as Dyer had written about. I felt nothing except cold.

The neighborhood seemed friendlier than I had imagined, though, so different from rural New Jersey, where Ashley and I had grown up. Where we had lived, you couldn't see your neighbor's house from yours and there was no sidewalk to stroll on. Here everyone had a short driveway and maybe a quarter acre of land, and their houses were built close to the street. It seemed you could practically see what people's plans were for the day if you just looked out your window. Were they dressed for a day in the city and running late for work? Or was it a thrown-on-rain-boots-to-drop-the-kids-at-camp-and-come-back kind of morning? You could probably see who had stocked up on groceries before the snow was due to come and who was finally putting on that addition out back. This wasn't the big city—New York or LA; when a murder happened in a place like this, I could imagine that it'd be quite some time before things got back to business as usual, if they ever did.

Tricia was murdered outside her home, in the house that was just around the corner from where I stood, only about a thousand feet away from the Gargiulo house. From local news clippings I had found from the time, it sounded as though after the tragedy, people had gone into crisis mode. The church where the Pacaccios went, St. Catherine's, had filled up, and counselors had worked overtime at the high school. Everyone seemed to agree: Glenview wasn't the sort of place where things like this happened. They all wanted to know: Who would do something like that to someone like Tricia?

In contrast to the way Ashley was written about, eighteen-year-old Tricia Pacaccio seemed about as wholesome as they come, according to the news articles. No one would ever call her a party girl. Everyone in town loved the whole Pacaccio family; it sounded as if they were like a Hallmark movie. The mother, Diane, was always in the kitchen cooking something, and Tricia's father, Rick, worked at Bell Telephone and was always kind when the neighborhood kids wanted to hang around while he was working on cars in the driveway. He'd show them the way the engine was put together and never lose his patience when one of them would inevitably do something careless. The younger boys, Doug and Tom, were bright and well behaved.

And then there was Tricia. She seemed to be one of those girls who did everything right, I read, but not in a way that made anyone jealous. No defense attorney could parade her sex life and drug use for a jury to see, as if it had some bearing on why she had been murdered. It just wasn't possible.

At Glenbrook South High School, Tricia had wended her way among the different cliques without belonging to any particular one. She was liked by just about everyone: the debate kids, the band kids, the straight-A students like her, she treated them all the same. She was pretty but not intimidatingly so. She had olive skin and wavy brown hair that reached just below her shoulders.

In photos from the various articles, it looked as though she had kept her style simple. She wore cardigans and jeans. For her senior photo, she had just a bit of lip gloss on and a pale blue top that almost matched the starry backdrop she sat in front of. She wanted to meet "interesting people who had the same desire as [she did], to save the world," an article said she wrote in her yearbook.

"Your strength, determination, and strong sense of right and wrong will see you through," her parents wrote back to her in a congratulatory message.

Thinking of Tricia as the "good girl" led to a bit of cognitive dissonance in me. I'd had in mind that all of Gargiulo's alleged murders had been triggered by a sense of sexual rage or jealousy. Tricia was so unassuming and demure—so young—how could she have been targeted? But then I realized how those labels—the hot one, the smart one, the good girl—were essentially meaningless. They were about how others viewed you and, maybe, how you viewed yourself, but they were not based upon any quantifiable truth. One man's hot one was another man's smart one, and if you were a murderous psychopath seeing the world through a distorted lens, you'd make anything fit one way or another.

I went to the Pacaccio house next, just at the bottom of a cul-de-sac. I pulled over across the street from the house and sat in my rental car, going over old *Chicago Tribune* clippings about the case that I had printed out from LexisNexis. I wanted to see if I could picture exactly how everything had happened back in 1993.

Some of the stories went into lots of detail about the night of Tricia's murder. Apparently her crowd of friends was doing a graduation party scavenger hunt, driving around the neighborhood looking for clues, all of them ending up at a big party. The concept seemed so quaintly dated, even though Tricia had graduated from high school only three years before Ashley and I did. Tricia was leaving for Purdue in a week, and the plan was that they'd cruise around and then meet up for a late dinner and party at T.G.I. Friday's, where Tricia's boyfriend worked. It had taken some organization, but they'd managed to plan it to fall on the creepiest, coolest date of all: Friday the thirteenth.

At the end of it all, it was after 1 a.m., and by the time Tricia got home, it was almost two in the morning. Reports conflicted as to whether Tricia had driven herself home, or whether one of her friends drove her.

Her father, Rick, usually got up early to take the dog out, and he was the one who found her body. He saw her tennis shoes first, pointing down toward the driveway with her legs lying limp over the second step of the side entrance. He fell to his knees on front of the stoop. Their neighbor Evelyn Kane was making breakfast in her kitchen across the street, and she heard the noise and quickly headed for the window. She saw Tricia's car in the driveway, and she saw Rick beside it, and then there was more yelling. Her brother Gerald was in town from Iowa, and the two of them ran out to see what was going on.

Tricia's legs and upper body were covered with dried blood, but there were pools of it around her body as well. Stab wounds covered her chest; one looked to be straight through the heart. Her arm had been snapped back behind her and was pinned under her back in an unnatural way. Rick was kneeling beside her, wailing still, keening almost. "Is she breathing? Is she breathing?" he shouted. Gerald, who knew CPR, checked for a pulse, but he knew it was too late. In a matter of hours, the neighbors came out, the police tape went up, and television crews began camping out on the lawn, the one I was staring at right now. It still looked partially green, even though it was near Halloween.

Years later, when I reached Tricia's friend Karen by phone, she still wondered at age forty-one: What if? In her memory, she had been the one to drive Tricia home, and through the years she still replayed the night in her head. What if she had gotten out of the car in the dark and walked Tricia to the door? What if she had waited to see that Tricia got into the house? "If I had done that, maybe she would have been safe," she said. We were quiet. I resisted filling the space with my own perspective. Don't do that to yourself, I wanted to tell her. I used to think like that, too. It eats away at you. But nothing was ever about just one moment, one false step, one trip to LA, one flat tire.

Instead I said nothing. I didn't want to cancel out Karen's feelings with my own.

"I envy you," Karen continued. "Going in there and trying to figure out what happened. When it happened to me, I felt like I was completely powerless and my job was to mourn."

I had never considered things that way: that asking questions and seeking answers the way I had done, as confused and overwhelmed as I felt most of the time, was something that another person might feel unequipped to do; that it took a sort of confidence, a sense of entitlement even, that I didn't often associate with myself but that apparently someone else could see.

An older woman looked out her window from across the street as I got out of my rental car. Could it be Evelyn Kane? I wondered if she knew why I was there. Perhaps she had a better idea about me than even I did about myself. She was probably used to people like me: the gawkers, the memorial makers, the people on the periphery trying to be a part of something. I looked down and tried not to be too conspicuous.

I stood on the edge of the property, nearly in the middle of the street, trying to picture how Tricia's body might have looked. There were the cement steps up and then a door that had since been painted shut, Doug had told me, but you couldn't tell that from where I was. The lamppost out front was covered by a large plastic jack-o'-lantern. Whose benefit was it for, I wondered? I imagined the Pacaccios had had it for years, pulling it out each fall to keep up appearances. Perhaps they did it for the neighborhood kids, because it wasn't their fault that a girl had been murdered on their street.

It was the saddest pumpkin I had ever seen.

•   •   •

Doug had told me that after Tricia had died, the Pacaccios couldn't bear to live in the house anymore, but they didn't want to sell it, either. The family had posted a reward of $10,000 for any information leading to an arrest, but nothing had come of it. They had moved in with Diane's mother, but Rick still stopped by the house from time to time to water the plants and mow the lawn. They kept Tricia's room upstairs exactly as she had left it. They didn't change a thing, even the "Sweet 16" poster that leaned against the wall, glitter glue letters sparkling.

Michael had been friends with one of Tricia's brothers, and after her death he had started behaving strangely. He'd sent flowers to the Pacaccios—other things, too, as the months went on.

Meanwhile, the criminal investigation continued. Police questioned everyone: neighbors, classmates, people who had been at the party that had apparently been going on across the street. Tricia's boyfriend was interviewed early on, but he was quickly ruled out. His coworkers at the restaurant said he was sensitive and well liked, and many attested to how hard he had cried over Tricia's open casket at the funeral.

Michael cooperated with the detectives when they came his way. He had nothing much to say, but in one interview he mentioned a friend of his whom he thought they should check out. Tricia's keys were also found lying next to her, and police picked up some DNA off them, but there wasn't a match on who it belonged to.

What Michael told Justin later that I heard about in the preliminary hearing—that the FBI wanted Michael's DNA because his best friend's girlfriend had been killed—actually wasn't so far off. Illinois authorities did end up pursuing him in LA in 2002 to get a sample. A match was made to some DNA found on Tricia's fingernails, but it wasn't clear whether that DNA was from on top of or underneath her fingernails, a key distinction in proving whether she had clawed

Gargiulo in self-defense, or had just picked up his DNA from casual contact.

By the fall of 1998, the Pacaccios had moved back into the house, even though no arrest had been made in their daughter's murder. Gargiulo was still around Glenview at that point, but I was never clear on what he had been doing in the ensuing years. Doug did tell me about a bizarre incident Rick Pacaccio had shared with him that must have happened that year, right about the time Michael was preparing to move to LA.

One afternoon there was a knock on the side door of the Pacaccio house, the same place where it had happened. Diane answered the door, and there was Michael. He wanted to talk to Rick, he said.

Rick wasn't home.

Michael said he'd wait.

And there he sat at the kitchen table for more than an hour while Diane tried to keep herself busy.

Rick came home in time for dinner. When he saw Michael, he didn't know what to make of it, but for a second he felt hopeful. Maybe they would finally get some answers. Just as Michael began to speak, the Pacaccios' side door burst open and in marched Michael's father and sister. They didn't even knock. They grabbed him by the neck, forcefully, and before anyone knew what was happening, they were gone.

What had Michael been about to tell the Pacaccios? They immediately picked up the phone to call the detectives.

That was the last time the Pacaccios would ever see Michael Gargiulo. Later that year he would land in LA, a fresh start.

I took a few pictures surreptitiously on my phone. I wasn't sure why, just that I wanted to add them to the file on Ashley in my desk back in Brooklyn. They belonged there, that much I knew. The house knew the truth, whatever it was.

.   .   .

I had now been to four different states and countless sites, trying to make sense of the loss of Ashley, and I felt as though the truth was becoming a more and more abstract concept.

Seeing Tricia's house, though, and Michael's, and learning about her story, made one thing clear in a new way: it can be impossible for some people—I was one of them—to ever truly move on when the truth will be always out of reach. This place knew the truth, the universe knew the truth, but perhaps the absolute truth shouldn't be a thing for us humans to obsess over. There would always be a new place for me to visit and a new report to read, but perhaps the truth was like an asymptote in geometry: I could get only so close, and then that final distance would stretch on as a constant out into infinity. Eventually I would have shift my focus from fact finding to letting go.

Half a year later, I sat with my parents in the TV room of my childhood home and watched Doug's episode of *48 Hours*. The title was "The Boy Next Door," and though it had its cheesy tabloid-television elements—synthy horror-movie sound effects, police sirens as interstitials—I viewed it without criticism, thinking of the compassion and sensitivity that I knew had gone into it. The Pacaccios were heartbreaking, and the childhood and teen pictures they had compiled of Tricia looked like ones any girl growing up in the eighties might have had—they looked like the ones I had. I understood that most people watched this type of show because they wanted to feel something. They wanted to connect to the victims and feel outraged that a killer was still at large. Sometimes the shows actually advanced an investigation, and sometimes they just made you feel a little more grateful for an hour or two. Sometimes that could be enough.

My mother gasped when Ashley's picture flashed on screen. I sat back, feeling a bit jaded. I knew how the sausage was made. Ashton Kutcher was mentioned, but I was pleased to see no mention of Ashley's drug use or stripping. Detective Small showed up, telling the interviewer that "the injuries [Ashley] suffered were horrific. Probably the worst I've seen." Justin, Jen, and Chris were all interviewed in a studio together. There was some jailhouse tape of Gargiulo as well, as the voice-over explained that he had met with the *48 Hours* correspondent numerous times while considering doing an on-camera interview. Ultimately he had declined, but not before telling her "My truth is being 100 percent innocent, being wrongfully charged."

Two months later, in July 2011, a man who had seen the episode and worked with Gargiulo as a bouncer in LA came forward to say he remembered he had heard Gargiulo bragging about having killed a girl in Chicago long before. That new witness was finally enough for a Cook County grand jury to formally indict Gargiulo for Tricia Pacaccio's 1993 murder. He would stand trial in Illinois following the completion of his California trial.

The show had done its job, on me as well. I was fairly certain now that Michael Gargiulo had killed Ashley, despite not knowing the guy and despite the lack of DNA evidence. But as soon as that realization settled upon me, I felt it give way to an even murkier and uglier question, one that I knew was probably impossible to fully answer: Why?

15

DIMINISHING RETURNS

I WROTE TO him once, a short query I typed out and printed on white paper from the office. I was squeamish about revealing my own handwriting for some reason—it felt scary enough that the thing I was touching would later be touched by him. Better to keep things as businesslike as possible.

I pictured the letter ending up in some prison mail room, being sorted and scanned by a warden before it was delivered by him. I wondered if my letter could end up with his defense team.

I rented a P.O. box at the copy place down the street so I didn't have to use my home address on the envelope. "I've followed your case," I wrote. "I grew up with Ashley and I'm trying to learn more about her life in L.A. I know you knew her." What a euphemism if there ever was one. "Anything you could share I'd appreciate." I understood that I was being far more polite than he deserved and that I gave the appearance of empathy. Internally I felt nothing of the sort. The gesture felt like a formality, a shot in the dark, some kind of due diligence just to be able to say I had tried. Gargiulo was a demented narcissist. I had heard him proclaim his innocence in the face of incontrovertible evidence. There was no reason to be had with him. I knew that whatever response I did receive, if there was one, would likely not even be intelligible, let alone sufficient.

In the movie version of this story, Gargiulo would have written back right away, and I'd be shocked by his sensitivity and humor. We'd develop a correspondence, and I'd find my emotions getting tangled in the unlikeliest of ways. I'd develop sympathy for him or a twisted affection almost against my will. I'd have to rethink everything I'd thought to be true. I'd have to rethink the person I'd thought I was. "What is happening to me?" I'd cry to my girlfriends, teary over whiskey in a dark bar. "I'm so ashamed."

Instead, I walked to the P.O. box every two weeks for nearly half a year and the box remained empty. Each time, after my heartbeat quickened and calmed again, I'd feel relieved.

After my six-month lease expired, I didn't renew it.

Meanwhile at Department 108, everything had started going haywire behind the scenes. Almost two years after the preliminary hearing, no trial date had yet been set. It seemed outrageous, and it was hard to find a clear explanation as to why. In May 2012, Los Angeles Superior Court Judge Sam Ohta approved Gargiulo's request to act as his own attorney. I read the news online at my desk at the office one spring afternoon and immediately excused myself for a coffee break. What was happening here? Was it good or bad? How could this be going on—wasn't it just the kind of absurd plot twist that occurred only in a movie of the week?

A short time later, Gargiulo would begin appearing at his many hearings as an official *pro per* (meaning "on one's own behalf") defendant, and an amateur trial blogger would begin attending the hearings and writing them up on her site, often paying for copies of the court motions Gargiulo filed and uploading them. The blogger's work was convenient for me, as I could read all of them from my couch in Brooklyn while drinking tea in the evening after work, although I could handle them only a few pages at a time or I'd feel sickened. I needed to alternate them with a few minutes of some schlock on TV like *Real Housewives*, something to remind me that life could be frivolous and madcap, not simply threatening and high stakes, careening between death and devastation and injustice every moment.

The Housewives are in Palm Springs, and there are tears and drunkenness and someone takes off her top in a pool. Gargiulo makes a motion to exclude statements gathered from him "through fear and coercion" during a secret jailhouse maneuver called the "Perkins Operation." One housewife with a tiny dog jokes about how infrequently she and her affable husband have sex. Gargiulo makes a motion to receive law library privileges in jail. I was hanging on to functional mental balance for dear life.

I would analyze Gargiulo's handwriting—his motions were now written by hand in a creepy, chunky lettering, alternating between capital and lowercase characters. Sometimes he'd stay between the lines, sometimes he wouldn't. I'd study the childlike way his *Y*s slanted down angrily to the left, the strange jaunty lean of his double *F*s. It felt bizarre that I should be able to get this close at such a remove, like how I had watched him in the courtroom from the back row.

His requests were commonplace and outrageous at once: one motion asked that he be allowed to have one hand free and uncuffed while in the attorney room at the jail—as a "high-powered" inmate, he is required to have both hands cuffed at all times when he is outside his cell. Another asked that he be allowed to possess graphic crime scene photos from the murders as part of discovery at the jail. The prosecution promptly filed an opposition to this motion, calling Gargiulo a "serial, psychosexual thrill killer who engages in the systematic slaughter of beautiful women because he takes sexual pleasure from it."

• • •

Later, I would come to understand that Gargiulo's *pro per* decision had likely been based on more than a narcissistic desire to call the shots. Lindner probably had a little bit to do with it—the two of them had been butting heads audibly in court, and Lindner was experienced enough to know that he didn't need to take it. He hadn't stepped down, from my understanding, but when Gargiulo had requested a new court-appointed lawyer after nearly three years of working together, he was told it was Lindner or *pro per*. He had chosen *pro per*.

For many defendants, I would learn, one of the most appealing things about representing yourself in trial was the privileges it afforded you in jail, namely, use of the law library, a computer, and the one phone in the jail that wasn't tapped by wardens. Even though contraband cell phones were commonplace, law library and computer access could still act as powerful tools when it came to protecting one's self from the violence and gang activity that went on inside.

Since a few days after his arrest in June 2008, Gargiulo had resided in LA County Men's Central Jail (MCJ), a Brutalist behemoth downtown built in 1963, just up the tracks from Union Station, next to the river. It was designed as a temporary holding facility for men awaiting trial or those whose sentences were less than a year, and in the past decade prisoner numbers had swelled enormously, making the total LA County Jail population the largest in the world and a nationwide symbol of the perils of prison overcrowding. A report by the ACLU called the place "a dungeon," documenting its "pervasive pattern of brutal abuse of inmates by sheriff's deputies" and calling for its immediate closure.

I had seen enough gruesome prison shows to imagine what might go on inside a place like MCJ: rape, riots, stabbings—sometimes even murder. The California prison gang system was well documented, too. There were four main groups I had read about: the Aryan Brotherhood, the Black Guerilla Family, Nuestra Familia, and the Mexican mafia or "La Eme," which was one of the biggest ones at MCJ. On the outside, the gangs ravaged swaths of LA and other California cities with violence, drug trafficking, intimidation, and extortion. On the inside, there was more of the same, plus jockeying for dominance and intricate systems of covert communication and honor codes.

Mexican Mafia members all knew the way to slip out of handcuffs; they had a way of whistling they would use to alert other inmates when a deputy came onto the floor; and they were all to carry a weapon or home-made handcuff key on their person at all times. They knew sign language, as well, and could instruct each other in how to build shanks and handcuff keys from common items such as an inhaler without saying a word. With Gargiulo's special status as a pro per defendant, he would have been in the perfect position to become a player for the Mexican Mafia, helping them carry out business and money laundering on the outside by speaking in code over the private phone; in return, he could earn their protection.

There was a new district attorney—Marna Miller had gone on leave— a new co-counsel, and a new court-appointed investigator for Gargiulo. The judge went on hiatus to appellate court—there was a new one in the interim—and then he came back again. I'd learn about each step from the amateur trial blogger or sometimes from an occasional group email that the district attorney's office sent to friends and family members of the victims. "Gargiulo Case Update" the subject line would read, and each and every time it would rattle me for a second, especially if I got it on my phone while leaving yoga or in the bathroom at a bar or in the middle of whatever regular life event I was occupying, floating along with my mind elsewhere instead of on the fact that I had a personal connection to a se-rial killer trial taking place across the country. Silly me.

The information the emails contained rarely registered as much as those first few pieces of news did, though. There were diminishing emotional returns on that kind of thing—mostly I had reached a point where the trial just seemed forever in the future, like an imaginary point in a faraway ocean that could never be reached in our lifetimes. We could talk about it and plan for it and get all our battleships in a line, but ultimately forces beyond our control would determine if and when we'd ever get to use them.

Still, I kept up with it all. Mostly because at this point, to quote Lindner, it felt like "the right thing to do." There were still a few things left that I wanted to see, wanted to hear, wanted to learn. I felt that at some point, my process—whatever it was—would arrive at some natural endpoint like a car slowly pulling into the driveway. It had to, right?

But what if it didn't? Where was all this information being filed in my brain? Was I knocking other things out of place to make it fit? Was I putting it into the "justice being served" folder? The "old friends" file? The "closure" file? It didn't feel like any of those, really. When I thought about all of that for too long—prison gangs, manipulation, all of us being toyed with by an alleged serial killer, the way Gargiulo appeared to drag things out and make us anxious for his next move, the way there didn't seem to be any way to stop him—I wanted to scrunch up my eyes and make it all go away. Would I ever be a person who didn't think of Ashley and her death every day? Did I want to be?

The fact that Gargiulo continued to exist when Ashley didn't felt outrageous. Sometimes it seemed that the world was a crazier and much more dangerous place than I had ever realized. Or maybe it just looked that way when I stared at it the wrong way: evil was deep and calculating and as unrelenting Homer's wine-dark seas. But thinking like that too long felt like getting inside the killer's head, and I couldn't let myself do that.

16

THIRTY-SEVEN POINTS OF SIMILARITY

THERE WAS, HOWEVER, a contingent inside the LA County District Attorney's Office that was making it their business to understand all the details I was reluctant to examine: trying to figure out how Gargiulo thought, how he saw the world, what views he'd had from his former apartment, how he had spent his days, how he might have chosen and "hunted" his prey, and everything that had gone on leading up to his alleged calculated plan of attack.

This sort of speculative thinking became even more relevant during the period when Gargiulo was *pro per*. Prosecutors often try to anticipate the arguments of opposing counsel as a strategic measure. However, during the *pro per* years, the potential issues were even more unpredictable. The opposing counsel was the alleged killer, who ostensibly knew more about the crimes than anyone else—because he had been there. A potential expert witness was dispatched on a multiyear project to visit all the relevant locales of the crimes and submit her findings. When the report was finally filed, it turned out to be very good news for the prosecution.

Retired FBI Special Agent Mary Ellen O'Toole, a forensic behavior scientist, had visited and studied the crime scenes of Tricia Pacaccio, Ashley, and Maria Bruno and the attempted murder site of Michelle Murphy, the woman who had fought him off. The report had delivered the opinion that all of the crimes had been committed by the same offender. This was huge, because Gargiulo's DNA was already linked to the Pacaccio, Bruno, and Murphy crime scenes, and now the link to Ashley's case would be even stronger, even though his DNA had not been recovered at the scene of her murder.

I read her assessment one night after hours at my office in a motion drafted by the prosecution that the amateur trial blogger scanned and uploaded. Technically, I read the *summary* of her assessment one night after hours at my office. It would take me another year to get through the entire seventy-six pages. It was another of those sensitive, potentially draining tasks that I kept saying I'd get to.

What was I afraid of at that point? What was left? I wasn't quite sure, but I assumed I'd know it when I saw it and that it was still ahead of me. I couldn't discount the idea that somewhere, at some point, I might still come across a certain fact or picture or quote that would knock me on my ass and leave me cowering. It was like the coroner's report all over again, but in many ways scarier. This time there was a living human monster attached to it all and a face I could attach to that. A face I been in the same room with and stared at for hours.

This was seventy-six pages of details on this killer's inner life. Seventy-six pages of his sexual perversions and appetite for violence. Seventy-six pages of the horror Ashley had experienced at the end. This was different from the crime scene photos I had thought I was prepared to see. Those had been terrifying, but they had been only the end result and had skipped over everything that had gone before. This would be all the tiny steps that made it come together. This would be "There but for the grace of God go I."

Maybe there were some things I still needed to keep in the abstract for my own well-being. Perhaps seeing catalogued in black and white the particulars of how Ashley had been chosen and then, once she was, how powerless she had been to stop the force intent on ending her—that was something I needed to keep at bay. Because what if it had been me? Couldn't it have?

Someone close to the case once described their perception of what Gargiulo was really like, not the version we saw in court or the version Chris, Justin, and Ashley might have hung out with years ago. The real Gargiulo, the psychopath mastermind, the one who could really be a cold-blooded killer.

This person had visited Gargiulo in jail, arriving unannounced. The high-powered floor where Gargiulo lived was kept dark—the inmates would put paper or cellophane over their lightbulbs to keep it that way, they told me. It was dank, too. You had to walk on the far side of the wall so that the prisoners couldn't reach out their hands through the bars and grab you. Gargiulo was sitting on the floor of his cell when this person arrived, scribbling maniacally into a notebook. He looked up from the floor; he was caught off guard, without time to put one of his masks on, and there it was. "I looked into his eyes and I saw evil," this person said. "It was chilling. It was not human. That's the last thing his victims saw. That's the last thing Ashley saw."

I picked up the report again on a Friday evening. I was still at my desk, killing time before meeting a friend for dinner downtown, and I had gotten into that strange vortex that sometimes hits you as an office worker. You've passed the normal hour at which you should have already left, yet for some reason, you can't move. Your work for the day is done, so why aren't you already outside? As you watch one coworker after another head out for the weekend, something mysterious keeps you fixed in your seat, until all of a sudden it is just you and the cleaning crew. Maybe it's boredom or inertia or muscle memory or the sort of sense confusion that comes from spending eight hours a day under fluorescent light. What was another few more?

I clicked over to the trial blogger's site. Updates on other splashy LA cases such as the Grim Sleeper dominated coverage. It had been more than a year since the O'Toole report had been filed. During that time I had been to Los Angeles three more times. I had met with deputy district attorneys and visited another of Ashley's favorite hotel bars. I had been to Vegas to Ashley's club and watched a man sharing my banquette get a lap dance from a bored-looking olive-skinned girl while his friend puffed on a fat cigar. If we were talking about the five stages of grief, by this point I felt as though I were somewhere in between bargaining and acceptance.

In the report there was a lot of overview to get through before things really started turning horrifying. O'Toole characterized the killer's crimes as "instrumental violence," as opposed to reactive or affective violence. "Instrumental violence . . . is a specific type of violence that is cold-blooded, purposeful, and goal-directed," she stated, whereas the other two types are more emotional and typically deployed in response to a real or perceived threat. Ashley's murder—as well as Tricia's and Maria's and Michelle's attempted murder—had been crimes of instrumental violence. "The emotional state of an offender engaged in instrumental violence is controlled." Controlled as in placid? As in how one might be pushing his cart down the aisle at Ralph's, considering a new brand of organic canned chickpeas because they're on special? Or controlled as if you're a serial killer and there's no need to let your pulse quicken when you're killing a woman because you have the whole thing orchestrated and timed down to the minute and you've gotten away with it before? Probably that last one. "This is an offender who does well in what would be extremely stressful and fearful situations for most people," O'Toole continued. Go figure—this guy sounded like a regular Tony Robbins.

The report maintained that the four crimes had been committed by the same person based on thirty-seven points of similarity, which O'Toole went on to define. Each had a header, ranging from "Blitz-Ambush Attack" to "Depersonalization of Victims" to "Post-Mortem Mutilation as Sexual Motivation." The killer was a thrill seeker. He "took multiple and significant risks . . . beyond what was necessary to commit the crimes. He likely engaged in risk-taking behavior to make the crimes even more exciting for him both psychologically as well as sexually." Among them: killing Ashley at her home with the lights on in a house that was visible from the street; giving himself a small window of opportunity to commit the crime (Durbin had just left her house—who knew if he might unexpectedly return?); and spending more time than was necessary in her home after killing her to mutilate and pose her body.

A note about the posing. In some ways this was one of the most grotesque elements of the crime to me even though I hadn't ever learned the specifics. The generals were terrible enough. The thought of it by itself was repulsive, that was clear, but there was a crucial gap in the information around the particular pose Ashley had been found in that had served to inflate things for me over the years. I had heard about it before, both that posing was a thing that psychopath killers did to their victims, and that it was a thing that had been done to Ashley. It was about depersonalization and criminal signature and somehow showing off your ghastly handiwork. I knew the gruesome details of how the alleged killer had mutilated and posed Maria Bruno—slicing off her breasts and nipples and arranging them in her mouth and near her head—but for some reason the details on how exactly Ashley was posed had evaded my notice. The posing had not been described in the preliminary hearing, and it had not been described in any of the preceding motions. I knew only that it had been vulgar and degrading. If I had seen the pictures back at the hearing, the mystery would have been over, but since I hadn't, I was forced again to speculate. Why were the horrifying details of Maria Bruno's postmortem pose referred to again and again while Ashley's were kept in veiled secrecy? Could hers somehow be worse? I found it impossible to imagine what could be worse than having one's chest ripped open, your own nipples positioned as if you were cannibalistically nursing yourself.

Was there anything written on Ashley? Had something been stuffed into her mouth? I knew that she had been found clothed and hadn't been sexually assaulted, so what could it be? My twisted ideas spiraled further downward. I held out hope that those visions would somehow end up being more outrageous than the truth, but I also wasn't sure why it felt it mattered so much, just that it did. Ashley had been brutally murdered and mutilated postmortem—how did that extra posing element change anything? I suppose it had something to do with the desecration element. That it was mockery and subjugation and twisting the knife into the living.

I had to wait until page fifty-eight of the report to learn more. Before all that I'd be treated to a veritable epic on serial killer behavior. The killer knew the layout of Ashley's house, because he had been there before. He knew the kind of street traffic that he might encounter on any given time of day on Pinehurst, because he had been there countless times prior to February 21, 2001. He knew Ashley's schedule and that of her friends, because he had observed her comings and goings for months—maybe longer—prior to her murder. Perhaps he had documented it all in a secret notebook, in a code, maybe like bird-watching or scoring a baseball game. *0800 large-breasted sparrow enters nest, 82 degrees.* In fact, this watching behavior might have even been part of his sexual motivation. Both Ashley and Maria Bruno were murdered shortly after having sex; the report attests that "This offender would most likely have been right outside their windows when this was happening."

Crouching in the bushes, maybe? Or perhaps camped out in the dog park across the street with binoculars? Or maybe he was the crossing guard that you pass every day on the way to your car. Take your pick of whatever fright-fest cliché you can think up—at least one of them was likely to be true. Picture the room you're in right now; maybe it's the kitchen, or maybe you're on the train. Now picture the world outside your frame that's just slightly out of view. Maybe it's the next train car or the outside of your house just below the windows. Now imagine there's a serial killer there, tracking your movements and counting down the days or hours until he descends upon you, but you wouldn't know a thing about it until it's too late. That was potentially Ashley's life for the entirety of 2001.

Of course one can't go through life worrying about a serial killer next door. Because then the terrorists win. Because statistically, what are the chances? What were the odds that of two little girls who grew up together in rural New Jersey, one wouldn't reach the age of twenty-three because she'd be brutally murdered by an alleged serial killer in Hollywood? What were the odds? You don't need to be a mathematician to understand that kind of statistical improbability.

I learned a new and disgusting word: piquerism. From the French *piquer*, or "to prick," piquerism is defined as "sexual arousal resulting from repeatedly stabbing a victim." I doubted it was something I would ever use in a sentence. *Could I get "Piquerism" for $200, Alec?* The report goes on to detail all the ways this killer had likely been aroused sexually by committing the crimes even though there was no evidence of sexual assault in any of the victims.

Chris once told me about a dream he'd had shortly after Ashley had died. They were having breakfast, sitting across the table from each other in the breakfast nook, probably at her house. She was wearing that pink angora sweater that made her look even more voluptuous than usual—Chris still had the sweater; he had picked up her last dry cleaning order. In the dream, he says, he asked her out of nowhere, "Aren't you scared?"

His voice breaks when he tells me this part, every time.

"No," she said.

Then he asked again, "How can you not be scared?" And then, in the dream, Ashley pulled up her sweater to reveal a suit of armor underneath her shirt. She told him not to worry. A metal breastplate, a cuirass, I think they're called? We smiled at each other wanly the first time he told it, at a big Italian restaurant in Pasadena one of the early times we met. "I just remember all the mornings we sat there and had coffee and talked about our nights before, whether we had spent them together or not," he trails off.

I love that dream. I love it for its hopefulness and convenience and naked neediness. I love it for the way it shows how the mind tries to protect us, how we cling to magical thinking and spiritual fantasy to cut through muck we can't compute and to try to make sense of terror. I wish I had one like it of my own.

Instead what I had was page fifty-eight.

There appears to be blood smearing between her legs, indicative of the offender positioning her legs. Her left hand with the index finger is pointed toward her inner thigh area and vaginal area. The blood pattern on the back of the left hand indicates it had been moved from the source of the blood where it had been laying. . . . Her legs are spread apart with her left leg bent at the knee and her right leg straight. Her body would not have naturally collapsed in this position. . . . For the offender, seeing these women displayed in this manner, destroyed and ruined, was likely very "satisfying" for him—even enjoyable, fun, and sexually arousing. He most likely wanted to remember them and how they looked and it is therefore likely he would have photographed them.

Enjoyable! Fun! Sexually arousing! Take that out of context, and you'd think you were reading about the newest couples massage treatment at your hotel spa. There is a sound track of a rushing mountain river behind you, and the masseuse is probably using ylang-ylang essential oil on your temples. How fun! How enjoyable! And how sexually arousing!

It was hard for me to square that the word *fun* appeared anywhere in this report. I wanted to put it back where it belonged: describing bike rides in the park and ocean swims and dancing at weddings. Then there was the pictures thing. Not only are there police photographs of this scene, now we learn that there are likely private ones as well. Where could he have gotten them developed? It was 2001, after all; there weren't digital cameras anywhere. I feel as though we would have heard if he'd had a darkroom in his apartment. Maybe there was some filthy place he went in the Valley that still developed snuff films; it was in the basement of some nail salon, and you had to know a guy who knew a guy to get in. Could he have had a Polaroid? Where are those pictures now? I think about some of the ones Ashley and I used to take, the preteen ones that got a little vulgar: there was some tongue wagging and crotch grabbing in oversized stonewashed jeans, with my pastel comet wallpaper as a backdrop. We were just playing around, we were just kids, but now I look at them and feel ashamed. It's as if we had been playing with toy guns, barely even considering them real, and then one of us grew up to be killed by an AK-47 in a mass shooting.

I think of Lindner's words at the elevator: "Sometimes that can turn out to be a lot to handle, knowing what happened." At the time I just wanted to get through the conversation and his sentiments felt trite, but now it seemed they were finally starting to sink in. Deputy District Attorney Marna Miller knew what she was talking about. It was indeed a lot to handle. Am I handling it? I think so. In some ways. Sort of. I think I am taking it in my hands and rolling it from side to side, seeing how it feels. I think the wet clay is leaving a sticky, muddy film on my skin. I think it will dry to a chalky finish and make everything feel tight. I think I will wash my hands later today as thoroughly as I can, and then still tomorrow I will notice that some leftover brown dirt has stuck around my cuticles, under the nail beds, and in the tiny fold of skin on my fourth finger knuckle.

17

NEAT LITTLE BOW

I WENT TO a weekend meditation retreat after a bad breakup. I journeyed to the Berkshires during a full moon and slept in a bunk bed in a room with a dozen other women. We rose at 5 a.m. and went to practice yoga and then to eat a vegan breakfast in the cafeteria. Each day we gathered silently for multiple three-hour sessions and listened to our Buddhist teacher instruct us in how not to think. Breathe in, breathe out. Fill your lungs. Notice with the out breath that it's possible to feel, very physically, a letting go. Direct your attention to the sensations in your body. Listen to your heart, and connect with what brings you here. Where are you holding on to stress? Where are you feeling pain? Where does loss live in your body? At every moment we have a choice, she would say. A choice to be present. A choice to respond instead of react.

In between our "sits" we would divide ourselves into smaller groups and share where we were in life. A man in my group started to cry before he even spoke. Another woman told of a medical ordeal so emotionally wrenching that I wondered how she could possibly ever leave her bed again. When it got to my turn I thought of Ashley, but instead I said something lame and self-protective about wanting to learn how to be more present and to manage stress. It was easier that way, or so I told myself, but I regretted it the moment the words left my mouth. Everything that came next would be pretending, and I didn't want to go on much longer like that.

Some of the exercises would involve staring intently into a stranger's eyes while the teacher talked above us in voice-over: "The person opposite from you has felt suffering. They've felt their body fail them. They've experienced heartbreak and deep love and seen the suffering of others." My partner for the first round was a woman who looked to be in her seventies. She had a scraggly white ponytail and was there alone and had brought her own meditation cushion. I wondered if she was somebody's grandmother. Mine, when she was living, wouldn't have known what to make of a room like this one. Doesn't anyone here have a job? she would have asked.

Our breathing deepened as we continued, the teacher's words floating around us like movie trailer narration. "The person opposite you has failed at something that was deeply important to them. They've watched a loved one struggle without knowing how to help." Even as her eyes began to soften in pain, my partner's gaze did not waver. I wished it would. She was too good at this. Her intensity would not let me look away as much as I wanted to. "The person opposite you has buried a loved one." Our teacher's words felt like punches in the chest, each one like having another item of clothing stripped off in front of this stranger. What would be left? It was as if I could feel the grandmother wordlessly appraising all the things about me she couldn't actually see: the stretch marks on my upper thighs, the scar on my left knee, the way my throat would catch when I thought about the very last time I had seen Ashley, on the downtown C train. How did this teacher know how to trigger protectiveness for all our hidden places? How did she know the things that made us cry out on random icy winter evenings when we slipped on the sidewalk? I had to fight the urge to bolt for the exit by digging into my tongue with my teeth.

There were many more sessions, more tongue biting, some vegan cashew flan, and a wish sent out to the moon. There was writing in a small journal and staring off into the mountains and wondering what lay beyond. There was silence and a new recognition of a perpetually searching quality within me that I had never fully acknowledged. That was it, wasn't it? The thing that made it so difficult for me not to pick at the edges, the inability to let things be, to replace one anxiety with a new one as soon as the first one abated, to resist comforting platitudes like "Everything happens for a reason," to ask the unanswerable "What if?" and 'Why?' over and over again, even on the sunniest of days. That was what made me not be able to let go of the unfairness of what had happened to Ashley. That was who I was, I had come to understand. Maybe it would have been how she grew up to be, too.

Perhaps it didn't have to be a thing I tamped down anymore. Perhaps I didn't need to see it as a flaw, or something that would automatically get in the way of happiness. Perhaps I could learn to see it differently; maybe it wasn't something that made me wrong. Maybe?

It was also here that I started thinking a lot about closure. Almost everyone at the retreat seemed to be wrestling with it in some way or another. It was as if they were speaking my language. Closure around Ashley's death had become my white whale. Maybe it would come if I just dug a little deeper, I sometimes thought. Maybe if I just read one more report, met one more friend of hers, saw one more site that was important to the case.

But in my quieter moments, I was beginning to wonder if it were even possible at all. What would it look like? What would it feel like? Would I even recognize it if I got there?

Over the years, I had gradually realized that the story of Ashley would never end. There would be no final note, no moment when things would be tied up in a neat little bow and stashed away in a drawer for safekeeping. There would be no time when I'd finally be sure I had learned everything or seen everything. There would be no startling epiphany, no lightning bolt to the head telling me "This is the ultimate *truth* about what happened to Ashley" or, for that matter, what it all meant to me.

There would be no precise time of letting go, either, no time when I could say that I had finally stopped searching for answers. The letting go and the holding on were happening concurrently, and they would probably go on that way forever.

What I had let go of, however, was the misplaced hope that closure could ever come from a trial or from Gargiulo's conviction. Closure, if it existed at all, was a state I had decided I could choose to embody at any time, like forgiveness or grace. By the end of the retreat weekend, I came away with a glimmer of knowing that one day, eventually, this might all shape itself into some kind of manageable order—Ashley, my breakup, all losses—or at least I could see a model for how it could be done. It wouldn't be final, and it wouldn't mean it wouldn't change, but it really seemed to be all about presence, as trite as that sounds. About facing my feelings and observing them without judgment, letting go of the wish for things to be a different way. Maybe it was the vegan flan talking. What might Ashley have made of all this Buddhist bunk?

I did believe everyone with even a little self-awareness was holding on to some wound or another somewhere, be it physical or emotional or both, and the trick of adulthood was learning to live alongside all that. Sometimes that project alone required your entire life. Sometimes it *was* your life. That seemed to be closure, or the closest we could come to it on earth. Maybe? I wasn't exactly sure how I would go about arriving at this peaceful living-alongside-my-wounds state or when it might happen, but I had unlocked some newly seeded faith—the closest thing I had to faith—that it would happen when the time was right.

Closure couldn't be based on anything outside myself, I knew that much. It wouldn't come from a conversation or an act, and it definitely wouldn't come from a legal proceeding. As I had learned more and more about the legal system—especially in a state that still had the death penalty, like California—I felt an incredible sympathy for the families and crime victims who were attaching their sense of resolution to a perceived finite ending that could be provided only by the courts. Trials were about the law, yes, but they were also about theater and gamesmanship and lots and lots of chance. What would your jury be like? How would they think? What sort of backstage dealings got crucial evidence withheld from proceedings that might have changed everything? What sort of police oversights could have colored the investigation? What witnesses might be lying on the stand? What tiny technicality or violation might result in calling the whole thing a mistrial? There was such a huge margin for error coming from all directions, and even after all that, a verdict was certainly not the same as the truth. At least for me it wasn't. It was a ruling, a decision by a group, an agreement on one possible explanation for events that could subsequently have a variety of consequences. Even if I believed in the system, I wasn't sure a verdict was the same thing as justice, either.

A footnote: Gargiulo's *pro per* status turned out to be relatively short-lived, and when it ended, the clock was set back all over again. He was caught holding what was possibly a homemade handcuff key in his mouth at the jail sometime during the spring of 2014, and then he lost his *pro per* jail privileges that had allowed him access to the law library and private phone, and a few months later, he gave up representing himself. Apparently representing himself didn't seem worth it without access to those extras, or maybe it hadn't ever been worth it in the first place; maybe it was just about control. His old defense attorney, Lindner, had been on standby and went back in the fall of 2014, and then for some reason the judge dismissed him again in 2015. What outrageous plot twist would happen next? It was a circus of unlikely events building upon each other with no resolution in sight.

Not to mention that Gargiulo will likely be in prison for the rest of his life even if he isn't found guilty of killing Ashley; there are simply too many charges against him in California, plus an entire trial in Illinois for Tricia Pacaccio awaiting him. And even if he is convicted, then what? None of it would bring the women back or even restore order in the world. There would likely be appeals. And more appeals. And what if he was sentenced to death in California? (There go those what-ifs.) Would the closure goal line be pushed back even further to seeing him executed?

That would be unlikely to ever happen, regardless. Besides, California has voted on propositions to eradicate the death penalty the past few election years, and since 1979, only 13 out of the more than 750 criminals on death row in the state have been executed, and the order of who's next to go appears to be determined at random.

When I broke it down like that, it all felt too unwieldy to get my head around, and I didn't want to connect any more meaning to the trial than I already had. I had decided Ashley's trial would be a reckoning, a coming together, and a milestone for everyone involved and everyone in attendance, regardless of the verdict. But it wouldn't be the end or even the beginning of a next chapter; there had already been enough of those.

Later, Chris told me he would feel as though we had failed Ashley's family if Gargiulo weren't found guilty. It was Ashley's birthday—what would have been her thirty-seventh—and we were toasting to her with prosecco and plates of pasta at a place in his neighborhood.

"I can't even imagine if that happens," he said, his voice cracking. "If I were her father, I would come to court with a fucking gun and kill him—I want to do that now." I moved my fork around nervously in my ravioli.

But Chris also had a much clearer idea than I did of what closure would look like to him; he had obviously thought about it a lot over the years. I envied that, and I hoped he would achieve it. "It would be some sort of acknowledgment from her parents," he said. "Like, 'Thank you for being such a great friend to her.'" We paused at that moment, the restaurant's up-tempo background music filling in the space between us. "I was. I really was. I was a great friend to her," he continued, stretching out the words for emphasis. "I can say that with all of my heart."

My friendship with Chris had started out a little rocky, but over the years since the hearing it had deepened into something almost profound.

When first I saw him testify, I wasn't sure we had much in common. Chris's grief over the loss of Ashley was still palpable—he put it in the room for us to witness and share, although really it didn't seem like he had much of a choice in the matter. His emotions leaked out of him involuntarily, like a physical process, like painful withdrawal symptoms rolling through the body from an addiction that would never loosen its grip. The carnality of it spoke for itself: everyone was devastated and shaken up by the crime, but Chris was the one who was heartbroken.

I was skeptical of his love for her and confused by its depth at first—he's this devastated, and he knew her less than a year?—but as time went by that morphed into something else, something murkier and harder to describe. Empathy, certainly, and some envy, too—if only my feelings for Ashley were as uncomplicated as it seemed Chris's were. If only my best memories of her were right at the end, instead of somewhere in the middle or closer to the beginning. It would be easier that way, wouldn't it? More painful, perhaps? But more normal as well, easier to prepare and season and cook and digest.

But there was also a vague competitiveness, a subtle tug to prove myself to him. After talking to him over a period of years, I would come to understand that we both craved a kind of recognition from the other. We were like war buddies, not from the same platoon but perhaps in the same region in different tours of duty. We needed a reference point in common to allow us to relax—"Was she like that with you, too?"—but before that came, there were other emotions at the forefront.

I respected him, regardless. Who knows how I would have appeared on the stand? Years later, when I'd be sitting in a windowless conference room at a government building in LA around a table with two district attorneys and two detectives, childhood photos of Ashley and me spread out before us, being pressed to share secret memories from more than twenty-five years ago, I would have my first glimmer of what it might have been like for Chris. How you try to hold in the tears because it's embarrassing to feel so vulnerable in front of passive strangers, but still they come. Not only for her but for yourself and for your frustration at having to express such delicate ideas about a person you loved to a bunch of men as they're taking notes. How much on display you are, how much pressure is upon you, and how scared you are of fucking up even though you're not quite sure what that would mean.

I see now that my skepticism about Chris's demeanor on the stand was about something else entirely. It was about different ways of grieving. Growing up into my thirties had shifted the direction of my grief: at the time of the hearing I was focused on myself and what it meant for me to be pursuing answers about my dead childhood best friend across the country in LA rather than staying the course with my life in New York. I understood now that the paths were intertwined all along.

The impact Ashley's loss had on Chris was commensurate with the feelings he shared with her—it didn't matter how long they had been in each other's lives or how I interpreted the way it looked on the outside. The outside stuff wasn't up to us anyway. I came to accept that the loss of Ashley had affected us differently because we had known her differently and we were different from each other, but none of that made either of us less false or more correct than the other. Whether or not we had anything in common as people, we would always share one essential part of our identities: we had lost the same girl.

18

THE DOG PARK

THERE WAS ONE thing I still wanted to see for myself, one place I hadn't been, one major site I had seen only in pictures shrunken down on my computer or projected large in court: the place where it had all happened.

Go to the dog park, everyone told me. The private one—though it was public back then—on Pinehurst across from Ashley's house; that was where he had gone to watch her. It was a few blocks from Gargiulo's apartment, an easy five-minute walk up Orchid, across Franklin, and around on Bonita Terrace. The pit bull he had paraded through the neighborhood was likely just used as a cover, a prop he could employ to pass as a normal man, when in reality—his own perverted reality—he was "gathering real-time intelligence" on his "target" and creating a plan. He wasn't just another guy picking up shit with a plastic baggie, knotting it and tossing it into the trash. He wasn't the same as that kind-looking balding single dad you saw from time to time with a husky and a flip phone from ten years ago. He was something much more insidious and much more terrifying to consider: a criminal mastermind walking among us. He was a Halloween costume, a horror movie franchise, a carnival ride with no brakes.

The dog park was gated and you needed a key, but I made it my business to find a way in. I was staying with Marisa again, having taken another few days off work to come west and hopefully put something of a coda on the past few years. I might just have to leave things on a big ellipsis for now, and that would have to be okay.

The trial was still ahead of me, whenever it would end up being. The years kept adding up, and new curveball delays kept presenting themselves, without a date even on the books.

I had traveled to the West Coast eight times since that first trip to see Oliver, and I knew now that there would forever be another thing to look into. Each piece I learned gave me a slightly different perspective on things, but I would never have the full picture. I saw now that I could make a meaningful endpoint for myself whenever I wanted to. I could choose a moment to take what I knew and who I was and how those two things overlapped, and I could sit with it. I could be present with it, I could hold it in my lap. I could simply let it be.

This trip would be my last one for a while, I resolved.

All of my research had served to give me a bit of a comfort level in LA, and for that I was grateful. Between visits to court and the sceney spots of Hollywood and the canyons I hiked while sorting everything out, I had developed an intro-level familiarity with and a twisted affection for the place. I had my favorite coffee place downtown and beach in Malibu. I had a modernist apartment I'd rent in Silver Lake with a deck where I'd eat avocado toast in the morning. I had a reason for being there again and again, and it wasn't about trying to make deals or being a starfucker. Something and someone in this place had killed Ashley, true, but that didn't prevent me from being drawn in, from being as captivated by its beauty and crassness as she might have been back when she had moved here at age eighteen.

Marisa offered to drive, and the two of us set off at dusk out of the hills on what felt like the beginning of a ghost story. We turned onto Hollywood Boulevard and then a jog over to Franklin, and within minutes we were there. Marisa was nervous with excitement—at having a new purpose, at the lurid unusualness of this errand. I was somewhat less so. I had been places like this before—I remembered standing in front of Tricia Pacaccio's house in Glenview for more than an hour—and I understood that, for the most part, it was rarely the catharsis you'd think it would be.

Ashley's house is a different sort of place entirely. A single-family bungalow set back from the sidewalk a bit, it sits atop a small, elevated lot with bushes and a few squares of front lawn scattered amid California native plants, green and burgundy. The paint job is pale yellow, and there's a gently sloping roof and an exposed cinder-block foundation. There are steps going up the side and a covered porch and room to park a few cars in front of a low cement wall, and there are streetlights all around, blazing down on Marisa and me as we find a place to stop near the corner.

It doesn't look like a party house to me, which is how it was often characterized by the defense. At least, now there's nothing flashy about the place, no bright colors or unkempt patches. No mangy dog chained to a fence, no motorcycle stickers next to the mailbox, no recycling bin overflowing with liquor bottles. "How many parties were thrown at the residence while you were living there?" I can still hear Miller asking Jen and her flat, exhausted response. How many people attended them? What were they drinking, and how did they move about in the world? It got so tiring to be typecast.

It doesn't necessarily look like a family house, either, whatever that means. The street does have a bit of a settled-down vibe. Could it have changed dramatically since 2001? Ashley was twenty-two when she lived in this house, and that's also hard for me to get my head around. Twenty-two-year-olds in New York—unless they had family money—were living in grubby railroad apartments or fifth-floor walkups next to an alley filled with garbage. Five hundred square feet of your own was a prize. What kind of twenty-two-year-olds had an entire house on a prime Hollywood street? Ashley had had a roommate, true, but also a front yard and a leased BMW and a place to park it in front of that. It was a world away from what my life was at the time, all chipped parquet flooring and subways and Chinese takeout.

"Do you feel her spirit?" Marisa asks almost immediately after we get out of the car. She's energized, I can tell. She's looking around excitedly, walking fast up the sidewalk and taking in everything around her with intensity. It's sort of sweet, when you think about it. She wants to take pictures and has offered to knock on the front door. I nix this plan, but I am touched by her enthusiasm. She wants to feel something, badly. She wants to feel a part of this.

"I don't think so," I say gently. I don't want to hurt Marisa's feelings. Internally, I'm less ambivalent. Of course I don't feel Ashley's spirit. Of course I don't feel bathed in golden light or sense the benign presence of a loving old friend. Is that really even a thing? How nice and pat that would be. How magical and healing and oh, so totally obvious. Why did I spend the past five years traveling cross-country and going to court and making people cry searching for answers if all I had to do was come here all along? Ashley and I could have been catching up all this time? Whoops!

And why would Ashley's spirit be here for me, anyway? If it were anywhere, it would be in New Jersey, in the woods, in my childhood bedroom or in hers, or at our school. In places we had been together and lived in and grown up in, not in this house that I had never seen before, where she spent the last and most painful night of her life. Not in Hollywood, not here, not on this street of agony and despair and injustice.

I take a deep breath. We are standing on the opposite side of the street from the house, staring at it as if we were expecting the crime to re-create itself in front of our eyes so we'll have something to watch. Nothing is happening.

"Ashley is here," Marisa says, sounding pretty sure of things. "She's saying it's OK." Oh, good. How lovely for us, and how cooperative of her. How fortunate for Marisa, as well. She should market her services as a medium.

I'm a little turned off by my own internal snark, but I can't help it.

The dog park is behind us, about a half-acre fenced-in lot with some palm trees and a little picnic table and chairs. It's locked, and there's no one inside. It seems unlikely that anyone will appear to let us in, and for that I am disappointed. I'd heard that if you stood in the very back, on a raised knoll near the fence, you could see directly into what would have been Ashley's bedroom and bathroom, just like the killer did all those years ago. We came at around the same time the murder took place—9 p.m.—so we would have that point of reference, as well. How dark was it, really? How many people were on the street? How many people had their lights on at home?

"It's welcoming," Marisa continues, outlining the energy she senses like one might describe a new neighborhood restaurant, all terra-cotta tiles and votive candles and house-made pasta specials each night. Of course my instinct is to brattily challenge her, like what if I told her, "Oh, wait, I made a mistake, it was actually that house up the road"—would she still say she felt Ashley there? Would Ashley still be welcoming us? What if I said, "Oh, yeah? What's it like? No, really, tell me everything. Has this ever happened to you before? Is it scary? Are you ever afraid the spirit won't leave you alone? What if you'll need to get an exorcism after this? How much would that cost? Could Rainn do it?"

But I say none of that. Instead, I let Marisa go on, just like I let Rainn go on, just like I'll let anyone go on who is feeling connected to this. I can use all the support I can get, really. Who am I to judge? Hell, maybe it's even all true. Maybe Marisa's time with Rainn has put her in touch with the spiritual realm, whatever that is, or perhaps she was a bit of a clairvoyant all along. Maybe I'm the only one cynical enough to want to cut people down who are feeling moved from the beyond. Maybe anyone else here would feel the same as she's feeling and look at me as the asshole.

I case the dog park fence. It's wrought iron and about four feet high, with spiky spires on top. Could we climb it? Would I rip my pants? Would it be worth it?

Marisa is across the street at the mailbox now. She's contemplating whether or not she should walk up the path, the same one Mark Durbin, Ashton Kutcher, and probably the killer walked the evening of February 21, 2001. She looks back at me, her friend of thirteen years, her friend who is trying to make sense of something, she's not quite sure what, her friend who has led her here. I wonder what she sees.

"Ashley is saying go forward," she says quietly. "She's saying this story should be told." She turns back to the door and falls silent. For the first time since we got here I feel a chill, starting in my shoulders and moving around down my legs and out across my knees. I look up at the sky. Muted music from the Hollywood Bowl is somewhere in the distance. We can almost see our breath against the streetlight. Is this what the spirit feels like? Do I feel it the way Marisa feels it? Whatever she just said, this message from the afterlife or from Marisa's subconscious gets to me as none of the others have. This is the one I want, the one I can't say out loud because it feels too selfish. Maybe this is what my kind of closure might look like—just as Chris knew he would give anything to hear from her parents, this is what I know I'd give anything to have. This is what I want to be true more than anything. I want to feel that I'm not trespassing. I want to feel that she knows I am honoring her, tonight and always. I want what can only be called her blessing.

A woman about our age or a little bit older appears, coming down the hill from up the street. She's with a dog, a big fluffy one that she holds on a leash. She is a benign presence coming toward us from the spirit realm, or else the cul-de-sac at the other end of Pinehurst. She is heading for the dog park.

Marisa is back next to me now, and we're both near the gate. Without exchanging glances we wordlessly shift our energy into mission mode. Our objective is clear: gain entry without arousing suspicion. The woman is next to us now, and she's pulling out a key.

"What a beautiful dog," Marisa says. "What kind is it?"

"Oh, thank you," says the woman. "She's a mix. Her name is Zooey."

Marisa bends down in front of Zooey, one knee on the sidewalk. "What a good girl you are, Zooey, what a good girl," she's saying, ruffling up her fur behind her head and on her belly. I've always felt a bit awkward around dogs, and for not the first time I feel grateful to Marisa for taking the reins. She knows what needs to be done, and she is saving me from my own overthinking.

"What kind of park is this?" Marisa asks, and just like that they're chatting like friends. I smile and nod and try to look like I'm with them, but inside I'm amazed at what's happening. In minutes we have gone from outsiders to almost insiders—our goal is within reach. Are there small dogs that come here? Marisa's asking. I'm not paying attention to details, but it sounds as though Marisa has invented a small dog waiting at home and an urgent need to find a new dog park for him since they're about to move to this neighborhood. Does the woman like this place? Is there a fee? It was the woman's husband that arranged their membership, so she's not quite sure who you call, but sure, yeah, come on in.

And just like that, the gates open before us. The door clanks as we step in and another chill sets upon me, but this one isn't about the spirit. It's about retracing the steps of the killer and the weight of being in the exact place to do just that. It's about mimicking the path that he took with sinister intent and wondering what that might confer upon me. Should I be carrying a talisman? Should I recite a mantra? I pause with Marisa and the woman and Zooey for a few moments along the center path, and then, after I decide that I've waited the requisite amount of time to look normal, I break away with a slow turn that I hope appears aimless. In reality, it is anything but.

I am heading to the upper-left corner of the park, that raised area. "What a good girl, Zooey, what a pretty girl you are," I can hear Marisa say in the distance as I walk uphill. I wonder if Zooey can sense what we're really doing here, that Marisa and I are both hiding something or that an alleged killer has been right where she's sniffing the ground. We know that dogs perceive things humans can't—that's why cops and detectives take them to crime scenes. What does Zooey feel underneath all that fluff? What sort of messages does the spirit send to a being with fur?

The grassy little hump at the top of the park does give you a vantage point clear across the street. Clear across the street into what would have been Ashley's bedroom. Depending on how the trees were trimmed, you might have even been able to see her showering. The killer and likely the investigators and cops and attorneys did this before me, and here I am standing in all of their footprints. The view from up there is a straight shot into 1911 Pinehurst. You don't even have to be much of an experienced voyeur to see inside. Am I seeing what they saw? There doesn't appear to be anyone home, but I stare nonetheless. I stare at what looks like a shower stall and imagine the killer standing in the same place, gaining "real-time intelligence" about Ashley as his body coursed with excitement. I think of how the people inside must have looked like dolls in a dollhouse to him and how that might have made him feel powerful. I stare at the lights on inside and think of all the conversations, fights, and mundane things that must have gone on in those rooms, then and now. Eggs, bacon, parking tickets, and water bills. Tears, shaving, watching the Thanksgiving Day parade, and years ago, a young woman was murdered. The house lives on. We live on. Or some of us do.

I feel something in between all that—in between banality and a sense of occasion, strength and resentment, inspiration and apathy. There is no power in standing across the street from where Ashley was murdered, envisioning and retracing the puppet mastering that led up to it all with no way to change the outcome. There is no power in being a woman whose first best friend was murdered. There is no power in embodying the male gaze that fixed on Ashley all those years ago in this space, a perverted version of the gaze she had probably felt for most of her life. But perhaps there is power in standing in all of that and realizing that I am here, bearing witness, and that I am not alone. The DA was here, detectives were here, Marisa is here—maybe Ashley is somewhere here, too.

I can turn my gaze away from this house. I can turn my gaze inward. I can turn my gaze up to the sky.

EPILOGUE

IN A LETTER to me dated October 27, 1998, Ashley wrote:

> How strange it is to think about the two of us living in great cities
> on opposite coasts. And also that what seems to be only yesterday
> we were digging through the swamp in your backyard determined
> to find buried treasure. I often think about how much I loved to be
> at your house, it was always quite an enigma to me. Nevertheless,
> remembering those times brings back a lot of innocence I know I
> have lost.

She was only twenty when she wrote that, and at the time I wasn't
quite sure what she meant. Not yet of legal drinking age, and already
such nostalgia. That was nearly a year before she came to see me in New
York, and I didn't yet know the details of the parties and the men and the
things perhaps I might associate with a loss of innocence in the practical

sense. Now I wonder if Ashley might have had something far less literal in mind. I wish I could ask her.

What keeps me up at night isn't the guilt or the what-ifs anymore. It isn't the whys or the hows that come upon me suddenly like an ambulance screaming down a quiet street. It isn't the unanswered questions about Ashley's final moments, either, or the fact that I never got to say good-bye.

It's all the years that have passed without her.

It's all the unlived lives that she didn't get to have. It's all the space between then and now that never belonged to her and all the things I got to do that she didn't. How would she have spent the last fifteen years? What kind of woman might that twenty-two-year-old girl have become? How would she tell her story?

It's 2016, and Ashley's been dead now for more years than I ever knew her to begin with. When I'm forty-three—which will come soon enough—she will have been dead for longer than she was ever alive. The absurdity of this thought never seems to fade.

What might have happened to our friendship? What might have happened after that fade to black on the train platform the last time I saw her? Would we have made our way back together by our midtwenties? Would Ashley be happy now? Would Ashley be at peace? Would she have her first gray hair by now? Her first child? Would everything have turned out the way we hoped it would as little girls?

I think of all the ways I've grown up since she died, all the ways I've been lucky, all the milestones I've reached that she never will: I've graduated from college; I've fallen in love; I've had my heart broken; I've made adult friends; I've become an aunt; I've felt loss; I've built a career; I've bought a home; I've fallen in love again. And all the while, Ashley is still dead, frozen in time just a short while after the turn of the millennium.

She's a Peter Pan in the worst way—the girl who never got to grow up. Her life belongs to the people who remember her now, the people who loved her, and the people who are fighting for justice in her name. We are the ones to tell her story. We are the ones who describe her and characterize her and look at her photographs and hold her in our hearts and minds as a symbol or a beacon or a parable as we move forward without her.

This past summer that truth couldn't have been clearer.

I went to LA with my new boyfriend in July. It was meant to be a pleasure trip. I'd see friends and go to the beach and show my boyfriend some of the places there that had become important to me: the streets and the hotels and the canyons and the bars I had traveled through on my way to learning more about Ashley. I connected with the current DA on the Gargiulo case, and we set a time to speak on the first Monday morning after I got to town. As soon as I got there and saw that picture on the table, I knew something was up.

My father had taken the photo with his old Canon from about five feet behind the piano at our first recital together; I recognized it immediately. It was Ashley and me from the back, sitting side by side in matching dresses the color of a pale pink rose in the Bernards High School auditorium in New Jersey. This copy was a bit grainy, given that the Kodak original from 1988 had been scanned and digitally transmitted and enlarged and printed out on paper and was now plopped down on a conference table at the Los Angeles County Hall of Records in the summer of 2015.

I had sent it to Deputy District Attorney Dan Akemon with some other pictures three years earlier by way of introduction—he had taken on the Gargiulo case after DDA Marna Miller had left in 2012—but it still came as something of a shock to see it again in that context. There were other artifacts spread out on the table as well: a printed-out map of Somerset County, New Jersey, where we had lived, with my town and Ashley's town highlighted in yellow. There was our fifth-grade class picture, too, with our faces circled in black pen. Emails the DA and I had exchanged from 2012 to 2015 were printed out, all of it sitting next to a file folder with my name written on the tab.

There were three other people around the table, too: Detective Small, from the preliminary hearing, and another attorney and another detective I had never met. Even before anyone started speaking, I knew what was happening: the Gargiulo case was gearing up for trial, and it was time for me to tell my story on the record. "You are an important link toward getting at the truth," Akemon said. "The stakes couldn't be higher." I nodded and I said I understood, and I did. I felt scared and accepting at once, a sensation I've been told is not unlike childbirth: you are experiencing a new kind of pain different from anything you've felt before, but part of you recognizes that what you're going through is natural. It is the appropriate next step in this course of events, and there's no way to fast-forward through it. All that's left to do is breathe.

I had the chance to help this legal team, and eventually a jury, learn more about the person Ashley had been, and my voice mattered, they told me. They asked me to speak during the penalty phase of Ashley's trial and said I could help them paint a picture of the life that had been lost and the way that loss had affected me. I would be a voluntary witness, not a subpoenaed one, but I was the only one who could tell the story, and suddenly it had great value to people other than me. With the memories I would share and the stories I would tell, I could bring her back to life.

Of course, of course, I said, even before they finished. I had plenty to say, plenty to contribute. I had been preparing for this moment for the past fifteen years, in a sense, and nothing they might ask me at this point could shake me, I thought.

They began to rattle off questions, the two attorneys taking notes as

I spoke. They would be the kinds of questions I might be asked on the stand when the time came, I was told.

I didn't cry when they asked me about the first time we'd met, and the things we'd liked to do together. What her childhood bedroom had looked like and what movies we had seen.

I didn't get choked up when they asked me about my last conversation with her, either, or the things we had done that week in New York.

I stayed composed when they asked about what pieces we had played in our piano recitals and if we had ever talked about what we wanted to be when we grew up.

But when they got to "What would you say to her now if you could?" I started to break down, perhaps because all the synapses in my brain were firing at once. What did they mean? Is she dead? Is she alive? Is it now? Is it then? I covered my face with my hands as I felt myself scrunch up into tears. I babbled something about how complicated female friendship can be, how your identity is shaped in reference to each other, and how growing apart can ache like the worst heartbreak. The three men stared at me and nodded in what looked like empathy. Inside I felt a gnarled jumble. We are all our experiences and all the losses and all the people we've ever loved rolled into one every day, I wanted to say. I would want to tell Ashley that she lives on inside of me and she will always be my nine-year-old best friend and I will always be hers even if no one else can ever see it.

I wanted to tell them how I think of that last moment I saw her on the subway—how I still think of it all the time—and how it contained everything. I wanted to show them how she looked when she walked away after we hugged and the doors closed behind her and I slumped back into my seat. I wanted them to see her walking toward the exit as my train began to move, how she had blended into the groups of people who had gotten off from the other cars and the ones who were still waiting there on the benches. I wanted them to picture the next moments I had never seen, just as I do, the ones I couldn't see as my train picked up speed and entered the tunnel: Ashley is heading for the stairs and then climbing up them to disappear into the crowds waiting for their bus inside Port Authority. If you were one of the people who had noticed her then—a beautiful young world-weary girl carrying a bag on her way to somewhere—you'd never be able to guess what had come before or what might come after. You'd never be able to tell that just a minute ago, she was sitting right beside me. You'd never be able to tell that we had started in the same place.

ACKNOWLEDGMENTS

SO MANY PEOPLE helped me along the way in the many years it took for this book to be completed. Thanks to my agent Larry Weissman and his wife, Sascha Alper, for their support and enthusiasm at the earliest stages. Deepest gratitude to my first editor Amber Qureshi at the late, great Free Press for her emotional investment, brilliance, and friendship, and to the dedicated editors who followed her: Alessandra Bastagli, Sarah Knight, and finally Karyn Marcus and the team at Simon & Schuster.

Thanks to my colleagues at *New York*, past and present, for editorial guidance, expert advice, and kind words at crucial moments, especially Jared Hohlt and Jada Yuan. Also Christopher Bonanos, Jebediah Reed, Kelly Maloni, Adam Pasick, Adam Martin, Rose Palazzolo, Jessica Pressler, Benjamin Wallace, Geoffrey Gray, Logan Hill, Mark Graham, Emily Nussbaum, Robert Kolker, Megan Creydt, Alyssa Shelasky, Molly Langmuir, Elizabeth Cline, and my researcher Jordan Larson.

Thanks to my friends, readers, and writing group members: Sara

Cardace, Emily Kramer, Caryne Hayes, Betony Toht, Joanna Rakoff, Allison Powell, Amy Rosenberg, Erin Hersey, Eli Marias, Lauren Feighan, Elizabeth Wildman, Amanda Patten, Michael Rothman, Jen Doll, Mary Kate Flannery, Mary Traina, Sarah Dohrmann, Glynnis MacNicol, Kate McKean, Molly Prentiss, Nell Bryden, Rachel Corbett; and especially to my incredibly insightful and supportive boyfriend, Thomas MacMillan.

Thanks to my LA friends, old and new, for hosting, supporting, and sharing your city with me on my numerous trips out west, especially Gianna Bourke and Charity Bustamante. Also Emily Foster, Matthew Lurie, Levi MacDougall, Joy Roberts, and Christopher Duran. Thanks to journalists Doug Longhini, Christine Pelisek, and Betsy A. Ross for sharing your expertise about the Gargiulo case. Thanks to Bernardsville friends and teachers for your stories and for helping to keep Ashley's memory alive: Rob Auten, Sarah Weaver Swolfs, and Alice Vuocolo. And thanks to my parents, for everything.

ABOUT THE AUTHOR

CAROLYN MURNICK is an online editor at *New York*. She received an Emerging Writer Fellowship from the Aspen Institute in 2014. Her personal essays have been included in *Before and After: Stories from New York* and *Lost and Found: Stories from New York*. She lives in Brooklyn.